The Touch of a Poet

The Touch of a Poet

Edited by

PAUL C. HOLMES

College of San Mateo

HARRY E. SOUZA

San Francisco State University

HARPER & ROW, Publishers
New York, Evanston, San Francisco, London

SPONSORING EDITOR: *George A. Middendorf*
PROJECT EDITOR: *Karla B. Philip*
PRODUCTION SUPERVISOR: *Francis X. Giordano*
COMPOSITOR: *V & M Typographical, Inc.*
PRINTER AND BINDER: *The Murray Printing Company*

THE TOUCH OF A POET
Copyright © 1976 by Harper & Row, Publishers, Inc.

Library of Congress Cataloging in Publication Data
Main entry under title:

The Touch of a poet.

   1. American poetry. 2. English poetry.
I. Holmes, Paul C. II. Souza, Harry E.
PS586.T6 1976   821'.9'1408   75-5446
ISBN 0-06-042869-4

Acknowledgments

Samuel Allen (Paul Vesey): "To Satch," from *Poets of Today,* published by International Publishers. Reprinted by permission of the author.

Kingsley Amis: "New Approach Needed," from *New Statesman,* June 17, 1966. Reprinted by permission of the *New Statesman.*

Hilaire Belloc: "Discovery," from *Sonnets and Verse* by Hilaire Belloc, published by Gerald Duckworth & Co., Ltd. Reprinted by permission of A. D. Peters & Co., Ltd.

Helen Berryhill: "Touch Tenderly." Reprinted by permission of the trustees for the estate of the author.

Morris Bishop: "The Perforated Spirit," copyright © 1955 by The New Yorker Magazine, Inc. Reprinted by permission.

Edwin Brock: "Five Ways to Kill a Man," from *Invisibility is the Art of Survival.* Copyright © 1972 by Edwin Brock. Reprinted by permission of New Directions Publishing Corporation.

Rupert Brooke: "Jealousy." Reprinted by permission of Dodd, Mead & Company, Inc. from *The Collected Poems of Rupert Brooke.* Copyright 1915 by Dodd, Mead & Company. Copyright renewed 1943 by Edward Marsh.

Gwendolyn Brooks: "To Be in Love," from *Selected Poems.* Copyright © 1963 by Gwendolyn Brooks Blakely. Reprinted by permission of Harper & Row, Publishers, Inc.

Carl F. Burke: "God Is Mr. Big, Real Big," from *God Is for Real, Man.* Reprinted by permission of Association Press.

Ralph Chaplin: "Mourn Not the Dead," from *Gathering of Poems,* published by Frank McCaffrey Publishers. Reprinted by permission of the publisher.

John Ciardi: "Gulls Land and Cease To Be," from *Person to Person.* © 1964 by Rutgers, The State University. Reprinted by permission of the poet.

Sarah N. Cleghorn: "The Golf Links Lie So Near the Mill," from *Portraits and Protests* by Sarah N. Cleghorn. All rights reserved. Reprinted by permission of Holt, Rinehart and Winston, Inc.

Robert Creeley: "Hello," from *Words* by Robert Creeley. Reprinted by permission of Charles Scribner's Sons. Copyright © 1962, 1963, 1964, 1967 by Robert Creeley.

Victor Hernandez Cruz: "today is a day of great joy," from *Snaps.* Copyright © 1969 by Victor Hernandez Cruz. Reprinted by permission of Random House, Inc.

e. e. cummings: "in Just— spring," copyright 1923, 1951 by e. e. cummings; "she being Brand" and "it is so long since my heart has been with yours," copyright 1926 by Horace Liveright, renewed 1954 by e. e. cummings; "r-p-o-p-h-e-s-s-a-g-r," copyright 1935 by e. e. cummings, renewed 1963 by Marion Morehouse Cummings. All poems reprinted from *Complete*

Reprinted by permission of the University of Pittsburgh Press. Copyright ©
1965 by the University of Pittsburgh Press.

James Hearst: "Truth," from *Limited View* by James Hearst. Reprinted by
permission of The Prairie Press.

Anthony Hecht: "The Dover Bitch: A Criticism of Life," from *The Hard
Hours* by Anthony Hecht. Copyright © 1960 by Anthony E. Hecht.
Reprinted by permission of Atheneum Publishers. Appeared originally in
Transatlantic Review.

Calvin C. Hernton: "The Distant Drum," from *New Negro Poets: U.S.A.*,
Langston Hughes, ed., 1964, Indiana University Press, Bloomington.
Reprinted by permission of the author.

Lindley Williams Hubbell: "Hour of Concern," from *Poems of War Resistance,*
Scott Bates, ed., published by Grossman Publishers. Reprinted by
permission of the author.

Langston Hughes: "Impasse," from *The Panther and the Lash: Poems of Our
Times* by Langston Hughes. Copyright © 1967 by Arna Bontemps and
George Houston Bass. Reprinted by permission of Alfred A. Knopf, Inc.

Robinson Jeffers: "Hurt Hawks," from *Selected Poetry of Robinson Jeffers.*
Copyright 1928 and renewed 1956 by Robinson Jeffers. Reprinted by
permission of Random House, Inc.

Erica Jong: "The Teacher," from *Fruits and Vegetables* by Erica Jong.
Copyright © 1968, 1970, 1971 by Erica Mann Jong. Reprinted by permission
of Holt, Rinehart and Winston, Publishers.

Shirley Kaufman: "Mothers, Daughters." Reprinted from *The Floor Keeps
Turning* by Shirley Kaufman by permission of the University of Pittsburgh
Press. Copyright © 1970 by the University of Pittsburgh Press.

Peter Kelso: "Poems," from *Miracles* by Richard Lewis. Copyright © 1966
by Richard Lewis. Reprinted by permission of Simon and Schuster.

Stanley Kunitz: "The Portrait," from *The Testing Tree* by Stanley Kunitz.
Copyright © 1971 by Stanley Kunitz. Reprinted by permission of Little,
Brown and Co. in association with The Atlantic Monthly Press.

Daniel J. Langton: "President Langton." Copyright © 1976 by Daniel J.
Langton.

Carl Larsen: "The Plot to Assassinate the Chase Manhattan Bank," from
Poets of Today. Reprinted by permission of the author.

D. H. Lawrence: "A Sane Revolution," "Gloire de Dijon," "True Love at
Last," and "When the Ripe Fruit Falls," from *The Complete Poems of
D. H. Lawrence,* edited by Vivian de Sola Pinto and F. Warren Roberts.
Copyright © 1964, 1971 by Angelo Ravagli and C. M. Weekley, Executors
of the Estate of Frieda Lawrence Ravagli. Reprinted by permission of
The Viking Press, Inc.

Don L. Lee: "Big Momma," from *We Walk the Way of the New World.*
Copyright © 1970 by Don L. Lee. Reprinted by permission of Broadside Press.

Vachel Lindsay: "The Leaden-Eyed," from *Collected Poems.* Reprinted with
permission of The Macmillan Company. Copyright 1914 by The Macmillan
Company, renewed 1942 by Elizabeth C. Lindsay.

Archibald MacLeish: "The End of the World," from *Collected Poems
1917–1952.* Reprinted by permission of Houghton Mifflin Company.

Naomi Long Madgett: "Her Story," from *Star by Star* by Naomi Long Madgett
(Detroit: Harlo, 1965, 1970). Reprinted by permission of the author.

1959 by Modern Poetry Association. Reprinted by permission of Doubleday
& Company, Inc.

Anne Sexton: "To a Friend Whose Work Has Come to Triumph," from *All
My Pretty Ones*. Reprinted by permission of Houghton Mifflin Company.

William Jay Smith: "American Primitive." Copyright 1953 by William Jay
Smith. From *New and Selected Poems* by William Jay Smith. A Seymour
Lawrence Book/Delacorte Press. Reprinted by permission of the publisher.

W. D. Snodgrass: "Mementos, 1," from *After Experience* by W. D. Snodgrass.
Copyright © 1960 by W. D. Snodgrass. Reprinted by permission of Harper
& Row, Publishers, Inc.

Wole Soyinka: "Telephone Conversation." Reprinted by permission of Mbari
Publications, Ibadan, Nigeria.

Stephen Spender: "My parents keep me from children who were rough,"
from *Selected Poems* by Stephen Spender. Copyright 1934 and renewed 1962
by Stephen Spender. Reprinted by permission of Random House, Inc.

Hollis Summers: "The Story of My Life," from *Seven Occasions* by Hollis
Summers, Rutgers University Press, New Brunswick, New Jersey, 1965.
Reprinted by permission of the publisher.

Jules Supervielle: "Full Sky," from *Mid-Century French Poets*. Reprinted by
permission of Twayne Publishers, Inc.

Sara Teasdale: "I Shall Not Care," copyright 1915 by The Macmillan Company,
renewed 1943 by Mamie T. Wheless; "Wisdom" and "When I Am Not With
You," copyright 1926 by The Macmillan Company, renewed 1954 by Mamie
T. Wheless; and "Two Minds," copyright 1926 by The Macmillan Company,
renewed 1954 by Mamie T. Wheless. All poems reprinted with permission
of The Macmillan Company from *Collected Poems of Sara Teasdale*.

Dylan Thomas: "Do Not Go Gentle into That Good Night," copyright 1952 by
Dylan Thomas; "In My Craft or Sullen Art," copyright 1946 by New
Directions Publishing Corporation. Both poems from *The Poems of Dylan
Thomas*. Reprinted by permission of New Directions Publishing Corporation,
J. M. Dent & Sons, Ltd., Publishers, and the Trustees for the Copyrights of
the late Dylan Thomas.

Reed Whittemore: "A Teacher," from *Poems: New and Selected*, University
of Minnesota Press, Minneapolis. © 1967 by Reed Whittemore.

Lionel Wiggam: "Grim Fairy Tale," from *The Honey and the Gall*, edited by
Chad Walsh, published by The Macmillan Company. Reprinted by permission
of the author and the editor.

William Carlos Williams: "The Artist," from *Pictures from Brueghel and
Other Poems*, copyright 1954 by William Carlos Williams; "This Is Just to
Say," from *Collected Earlier Poems*, copyright 1938 by William Carlos
Williams. Reprinted by permission of New Directions Publishing Corporation.

William Butler Yeats: "A Deep-Sworn Vow," copyright 1919 by The
Macmillan Company, renewed 1947 by Bertha Georgie Yeats; "For Anne
Gregory," copyright 1933 by The Macmillan Company, renewed 1961 by
Bertha Georgie Yeats; and "When You Are Old," copyright 1906 by The
Macmillan Company, renewed 1934 by William Butler Yeats. All poems are
from *Collected Poems of William Butler Yeats*. Reprinted by permission of
The Macmillan Company, M. B. Yeats, Miss Anne Yeats, and Macmillan
of London & Basingstoke.

Photography Credits

Below are listed the pages on which photographs appear. We appreciate the right to reproduce the following photographs.

To
Anna, Carmel, Judy, and Nanoe

Contents

Harsh

Light

Heavy

Sensorium

Handbook

Gentle

Harsh

Light

Sensorium   271

Preface

Several years ago, I started encouraging my students to select poems that touched them emotionally and that they had particularly enjoyed reading and discussing in class. What began as a small collection of poems gradually grew into an avalanche of poetry. Having always been a firm believer in student participation in curriculum development, I hit on the idea of compiling an anthology of poems chosen by students and the instructor. I later decided that the addition of photographs would help a visually oriented generation respond to the poems and recognize more readily that poetry is also a form of imagery.

Furthermore, I decided that my coeditors should be college students. I chose Harry E. Souza, a graduate student and personal friend of mine, because of his great love of and feel for poetry. In addition to the poems chosen by my students, Harry and I went through hundreds of poetry collections and picked out poems we thought students could relate to and enjoy. As coeditor for the *Handbook*, I chose Joey Tranchina, a graduate English student, poet, and professional photographer. We agreed that we wanted a unique and informal handbook which would stimulate and encourage students to respond to the poetry anthology.

We would have been unable to finish this book without the help of the following students: Sammi Gavich, Faith Beebe, Gayle Digiovanni, Colleen Sullivan, Debbie Zitrin, Curtis Lindskog, Rose Shirinian, David Stone, and too many others to list in this limited space; and fellow faculty members: Helen Berryhill, Jean Pumphrey, John Cafferata, Louise Hazelton, Jack Gill, and Barbara Mertes. Our special thanks go to our excellent manuscript typist, Harriet Saign, and to Douglas Echols for all of his help and suggestions in preparing the manuscript.

P.C.H.

To the Student

Since the poetic experience is one in which the poet conveys an impression from his own life to that of the reader, the reading of a poem should be thought of as an expansion of one's self into the world of another—a world that will hopefully not only stimulate one's thoughts but also arouse one's feelings.

Now, how do you enter the poet's world? First, I suggest reading the poems aloud rather than limiting your experience to silent readings. Second, explore each poem thoroughly. Start your journey of exploration by asking the following questions: What mood or feeling does the poem create for me? What lines are most effective? What does the poem make me think about or feel? View the poem from every conceivable vantage point, but most of all be willing to enter the poet's world with an open mind. Third, react to the poem. Which words or phrases created feelings or mental pictures for you? How did your mood or mental set affect your interpretation and/or reaction to the poet's experience? Fourth, write down your reactions to the poem as they occur to you.

I hope these few suggestions will help you gain a fuller impression of the poet and his world and help make poetry a pleasure rather than a chore.

P.C.H.

To the Instructor

... they should see with their eyes
Hear with their ears
Understand with their hearts.
Matthew 13:15

The poems selected for this anthology were specifically chosen by College of San Mateo students, Harry Souza, and me to help all student readers to both experience and respond emotionally to poetry. Far too often many instructors insist that the form of poetry is of first importance. When students do not recognize the form, the instructors unfortunately conclude that there is nothing more worth discussing. In addition, much of the apparatus included in many poetry books overemphasizes explication and terminology, thus creating artificial barriers between the reader and what the poet is trying to tell him or make him feel. Consequently, students erroneously conclude that all poetry is basically an intellectual rather than emotional experience.

Since a poem is an indication of how a sensitive member of a society imagines, dreams, thinks, and feels, it should not be taught solely as a problem or puzzle to be solved or deciphered. Instead, students should be encouraged to *feel* or *experience* something when they read a particular poem. They should initially make a sensory exploration of the poem; then they should attempt to discover and spontaneously express in their *own* words what they feel (not necessarily what the instructor thinks they should feel). The study of the craft of poetry can be pursued at a later time with the assistance of the instructor and the handbook. By stressing imagery as the basic element of poetry, an instructor should be able to motivate his students to express what sights, sounds, or feelings a poem elicits.

Realizing that it is difficult (if not almost impossible) to put poems into rigid categories, we nevertheless decided, for expediency's sake, to divide the poems in this anthology into four arbitrary divisions:

GENTLE — poems that reflect the beauty of man, life, love, nature, and so forth as perceived by the poet
HARSH — poems that contain a cynical or caustic comment on life, love, man, society, morals, and the like
LIGHT — poems that usually contain a humorous, witty, or satirical comment on human activity or some weakness of human nature

HEAVY — poems that require several readings and provoke serious thought, feeling, and consideration about the human experience

All four of these classifications can refer to some type of touching, and we encourage the students to keep this in mind while reading the poems. Gentle, Harsh, Light, and Heavy reflect the various tones or moods of the poems contained in this anthology, and it is in the general area of exploring these tones and moods that instructors can assist the students. We also recognized that there are various degrees of lightness as well as seriousness; we know that no matter what the subject or the form, the poet may direct his mood or tone toward something in between which borrows from both extremes. Therefore, the categories Gentle, Harsh, Light, and Heavy are used only to assist students and instructors in exploring the range of emotions expressed in the poems.

Hopefully, the poems in this anthology will stimulate students to explore and experience other poems. And perhaps eventually they will come to believe that "any person who ignores poetry risks isolation from the most important ideas of his time."

P.C.H.

The Touch of a Poet

Read the poems you like reading. Don't bother whether they're "important," or if they'll live. What does it matter what poetry *is*, after all? If you want a definition of poetry, say: "Poetry is what makes me laugh or cry or yawn, what makes my toenails twinkle, what makes me want to do this or that or nothing," and let it go at that. All that matters about poetry is the enjoyment of it, however tragic it may be. All that matters is the eternal movement behind it, the vast undercurrent of human grief, folly, pretension, exaltation, or ignorance, however unlofty the intention of the poem.

Dylan Thomas
Notes on the Art of Poetry

Introduction:
The Poet Speaks

Meaning is of the intellect, poetry is not . . .
Poetry [is] more physical than intellectual. . . .
To transfuse emotion—not to transmit thought but to
set up in the reader's sense a vibration corresponding
to what was felt by the writer—is the peculiar
function of poetry. *A. E. Housman*

My photographs are gifts and I am always glad
when they have touched people. *Nell Dorr*

Lawrence Ferlinghetti   *Allen Ginsberg*

Constantly Risking Absurdity

Lawrence Ferlinghetti

Constantly risking absurdity
          and death
   whenever he performs
        above the heads
           of his audience
the poet like an acrobat
       climbs on rime
         to a high wire of his own making
and balancing on eyebeams
        above a sea of faces
    paces his way
       to the other side of day
   performing entrechats
        and sleight-of-foot tricks
and other high theatrics
        and all without mistaking
     any thing
        for what it may not be
  For he's the super realist
        who must perforce perceive
    taut truth
       before the taking of each stance or step
in his supposed advance
       toward that still higher perch
  where Beauty stands and waits
       with gravity
        to start her death-defying leap
And he
   a little charleychaplin man
       who may or may not catch
   her fair eternal form
       spreadeagled in the empty air
    of existence

Poems

Peter Kelso (Age 11)

In poems, our earth's wonders
Are windowed through
>   Words

A good poem must haunt the heart
And be heeded by the head of the
>   Hearer

With a wave of words, a poet can
Change his feelings into cool, magical, mysterious
>   Mirages

Without poetry our world would be
Locked within itself—no longer enchanted by the poet's
>   Spell.

Poetry

Marianne Moore

I, too, dislike it: there are things that are important beyond
      all this fiddle.
  Reading it, however, with a perfect contempt for it, one
      discovers in
  it, after all, a place for the genuine.
     Hands that can grasp, eyes
      that can dilate, hair that can rise
         if it must, these things are important not because a

high-sounding interpretation can be put upon them but be-
         cause they are
   useful. When they become so derivative as to become un-
      intelligible,
  the same thing may be said for all of us, that we
     do not admire what
     we cannot understand: the bat
        holding on upside down or in quest of something to

eat, elephants pushing, a wild horse taking a roll, a tireless
      wolf under
  a tree, the immovable critic twitching his skin like a horse
      that feels a flea, the base-
  ball fan, the statistician—
     nor is it valid
      to discriminate against "business documents and

school-books"; all these phenomena are important. One must
      make a distinction
  however: when dragged into prominence by half poets, the
      result is not poetry,
  nor till the poets among us can be
     "literalists of
     the imagination "—above
        insolence and triviality and can present

for inspection, "imaginary gardens with real toads in them,"
      shall we have
  it. In the meantime, if you demand on the one hand,
  the raw material of poetry in
     all its rawness and
     that which is on the other hand
        genuine, you are interested in poetry.

Poetry Liberation

Jean Pumphrey

Poetry, sir,
is essence,
you say,
and monkeys
with little jackets
in the rain.
Poetry, you say,
is charm,
"She dips her fingers
in the pool
without a ripple,
lifts them dry."
Art, then,
is life upon the shelf,
not flesh.
You range
from classic Greek
to Japanese
without a ripple,
carving
delicate cameos
of Plato and Haiku,
art without history,
polished, pale,
as the lady poetry
gallops away.

In My Craft or Sullen Art

Dylan Thomas

In my craft or sullen art
Exercised in the still night
When only the moon rages
And the lovers lie abed
With all their griefs in their arms,
I labour by singing light
Not for ambition or bread
Or the strut and trade of charms
On the ivory stages
But for the common wages
Of their most secret heart.

Not for the proud man apart
From the raging moon I write
On these spindrift pages
Nor for the towering dead
With their nightingales and psalms
But for the lovers, their arms
Round the griefs of the ages,
Who pay no praise or wages
Nor heed my craft or art.

Gentle

Touch Tenderly

Helen Berryhill

Touch tenderly
When you touch—
If you touch—
For you will touch timidity
And fold a fluttering in your hands.

Hold
This frightened fawn
Meadowed in your grasp,
Enfold
This quivering leaf
Air-borne in your press.

Handle
Immortality
Denying all of death,
Fondle
Eternity
Acclaiming all of breath.

But oh, touch tenderly
When you touch—
If you touch—
For you will touch fragility
And hold rare dream-stuff in your hands.

Sonnet 18

William Shakespeare

Shall I compare thee to a summer's day?
Thou art more lovely and more temperate:
Rough winds do shake the darling buds of May,
And summer's lease hath all too short a date:
Sometime too hot the eye of heaven shines,
And often is his gold complexion dimmed;
And every fair from fair sometime declines,
By chance, or nature's changing course, untrimmed;
But thy eternal summer shall not fade
Nor lose possession of that fair thou ow'st,
Nor shall Death brag thou wand'rest in his shade
When in eternal lines to time thou grow'st.
    So long as men can breathe or eyes can see,
    So long lives this, and this gives life to thee.

This Is Just To Say

William Carlos Williams

I have eaten
the plums
that were in
the icebox

and which
you were probably
saving
for breakfast

Forgive me
they were delicious
so sweet
and so cold

A Jellyfish

Marianne Moore

Visible, invisible,
    a fluctuating charm
an amber-tinctured amethyst
    inhabits it, your arm
approaches and it opens
    and it closes; you had meant
to catch it and it quivers;
    you abandon your intent.

The Touch of a Poet

To Be in Love

Gwendolyn Brooks

To be in love
Is to touch things with a lighter hand.

In yourself you stretch, you are well.

You look at things
Through his eyes.
A Cardinal is red.
A sky is blue.
Suddenly you know he knows too.
He is not there but
You know you are tasting together
The winter, or light spring weather.

His hand to take your hand is overmuch.
Too much to bear.

You cannot look in his eyes
Because your pulse must not say
What must not be said.

When he
Shuts a door—
Is not there—
Your arms are water.

And you are free
With a ghastly freedom.

You are the beautiful half
Of a golden hurt.

You remember and covet his mouth,
To touch, to whisper on.

Oh when to declare
Is certain Death!

Oh when to apprize
Is to mesmerize,

To see fall down, the Column of Gold,
Into the commonest ash.

in Just—   spring

e. e. cummings

in Just-
spring   when the world is mud-
luscious the little
lame balloonman

whistles   far   and wee

and eddieandbill come
running from marbles and
piracies and it's
spring

when the world is puddle-wonderful

the queer
old balloonman whistles
far   and   wee
and bettyandisbel come dancing

from hop-scotch and jump-rope and

it's
spring
and
    the
        goat-footed
balloonMan   whistles
far
and
wee

Sonnet 29

William Shakespeare

When in disgrace with Fortune and men's eyes,
I all alone beweep my outcast state,
And trouble deaf heaven with my bootless cries,
And look upon myself and curse my fate,
Wishing me like to one more rich in hope,
Featured like him, like him with friends possessed,
Desiring this man's art and that man's scope,
With what I most enjoy contented least;
Yet in these thoughts myself almost despising,
Haply I think on thee, and then my state,
Like to the lark at break of day arising
From sullen earth, sings hymns at heaven's gate;
    For thy sweet love rememb'red such wealth brings
    That then I scorn to change my state with kings.

I Saw in Louisiana a Live-Oak Growing

Walt Whitman

I saw in Louisiana a live-oak growing,
All alone stood it, and the moss hung down from the branches;
Without any companion it grew there uttering joyous leaves
    of dark green,
And its look, rude, unbending, lusty, made me think of myself;
But I wonder'd how it could utter joyous leaves standing alone there,
    without its friend, its lover near—for I knew I could not;
And I broke off a twig with a certain number of leaves upon it, and
    twined around it a little moss,
And brought it away—and I have placed it in sight in my room,
It is not needed to remind me as of my own dear friends,
(For I believe lately I think of little else than of them:)
Yet it remains to me a curious token—it makes me think of manly love;
For all that, and though the live-oak glistens there in Louisiana,
    solitary in a wide flat space,
Uttering joyous leaves all its life, without a friend, a lover, near,
I know very well I could not.

When I Am Not With You

Sara Teasdale

When I am not with you
I am alone,
For there is no one else
And there is nothing
That comforts me but you.
When you are gone
Suddenly I am sick,
Blackness is round me,
There is nothing left.
I have tried many things,
Music and cities,
Stars in their constellations
And the sea,
But there is nothing
That comforts me but you;
And only poor pride bows down
Like grass in a rain-storm
Drenched with my longing.
The night is unbearable,
Oh let me go to you.
For there is no one,
There is nothing
To comfort me but you.

Where Have You Gone?

Mari E. Evans

Where have you gone

with your confident
walk with
your crooked smile

why did you leave
me
when you took your
laughter
and departed

are you aware that
with you
went the sun
all light
and what few stars
there were?

where have you gone
with your confident
walk your
crooked smile the
rent money
in one pocket and
my heart
in another . . .

The River-Merchant's Wife: A Letter

Ezra Pound

While my hair was still cut straight across my forehead
I played about the front gate, pulling flowers.
You came by on bamboo stilts, playing horse,
You walked about my seat, playing with blue plums.
And we went on living in the village of Chokan:
Two small people, without dislike or suspicion.

At fourteen I married My Lord you.
I never laughed, being bashful.
Lowering my head, I looked at the wall.
Called to, a thousand times, I never looked back.

At fifteen I stopped scowling,
I desired my dust to be mingled with yours
Forever and forever and forever.
Why should I climb the look out?

At sixteen you departed,
You went into far Ku-to-yen, by the river of swirling eddies,
And you have been gone five months.
The monkeys make sorrowful noise overhead.

You dragged your feet when you went out.
By the gate now, the moss is grown, the different mosses,
Too deep to clear them away!
The leaves fall early this autumn, in wind.
The paired butterflies are already yellow with August
Over the grass in the West garden;
They hurt me. I grow older.
If you are coming down through the narrows of the river Kiang,
Please let me know beforehand,
And I will come out to meet you
                    As far as Cho-fu-sa.

My Heart Leaps Up

William Wordsworth

My heart leaps up when I behold
    A rainbow in the sky:
So was it when my life began;
So is it now I am a man;
So be it when I shall grow old,
    Or let me die!
The Child is father of the Man;
And I could wish my days to be
Bound each to each by natural piety.

In a Station of the Metro

Ezra Pound

The apparition of these faces in the crowd;
Petals on a wet, black bough.

Afterwards

Thomas Hardy

When the Present has latched its postern behind my tremulous stay,
    And the May month flaps its glad green leaves like wings,
Delicate-filmed as new-spun silk, will the neighbors say,
    "He was a man who used to notice such things"?

If it be in the dusk when, like an eyelid's soundless blink,
    The dewfall-hawk comes crossing the shades to alight
Upon the wind-warped upland thorn, a gazer may think,
    "To him this must have been a familiar sight."

If I pass during some nocturnal blackness, mothy and warm,
    When the hedgehog travels furtively over the lawn,
One may say, "He strove that such innocent creatures should come
        to no harm,
    But he could do little for them; and now he is gone."

If, when hearing that I have been stilled at last, they stand at the door,
    Watching the full-starred heavens that winter sees,
Will this thought rise on those who will meet my face no more,
    "He was one who had an eye for such mysteries"?

And will any say when my bell of quittance is heard in the gloom,
    And a crossing breeze cuts a pause in its outrollings,
Till they rise again, as they were a new bell's boom,
    "He hears it not now, but used to notice such things"?

Two Minds

Sara Teasdale

Your mind and mine are such great lovers they
Have freed themselves from cautious human clay,
And on wild clouds of thought, naked together
They ride above us in extreme delight;
We see them, we look up with a lone envy
And watch them in their zone of crystal weather
That changes not for winter or the night.

The Mounting Summer, Brilliant and Ominous

Delmore Schwartz

A yellow-headed, gold-hammered, sunflower-lanterned
Summer afternoon: after the sun soared
All morning to the marble-shining heights of the marvellous blue
Like lions insurgent, bursting out of a great black zoo,
As if all radiance rode over and roved and dove
To the thick dark night where the fluted roots clutched and grasped
As if all vividness poured, out poured
Over, bursting and falling and breaking,
As when the whole ocean rises and rises, in irresistible, uncontrollable
　　motion, shaking:
The roar of the heart in a shell and the roar of the sea beyond the
　　concessions of possession and the successions of time's continual
　　procession.

Any Man's Advice to His Son

Kenneth Fearing

If you have lost the radio beam, then guide yourself by the sun or the
   stars.
(By the North Star at night, and in daytime by the compass and the
   sun.)
Should the sky be overcast and there are neither stars nor a sun, then
   steer by dead reckoning.
If the wind and direction and speed are not known, then trust to your
   wits and your luck.

Do you follow me? Do you understand? Or is this too difficult to learn?
But you must and you will, it is important that you do,
Because there may be troubles even greater than these that I have said.

Because, remember this: Trust no man fully.
Remember: If you must shoot at another man, squeeze, do not jerk the
   trigger. Otherwise you may miss and die, yourself, at the hand of
   some other man's son.
And remember: In all this world there is nothing so easily squandered,
   or once gone, so completely lost as life.

I tell you this because I remember you when you were small,
And because I remember all your monstrous infant boasts and lies,
And the way you smiled, and how you ran and climbed, as no one else
   quite did, and how you fell and were bruised,
And because there is no other person, anywhere on earth, who
   remembers these things as clearly as I do now.

I'd Want Her Eyes
to Fill with Wonder

Kenneth Patchen

I'd want her eyes to fill with wonder
I'd want her lips to open just a little
I'd want her breasts to lift at my touch

And O I'd tell her that I loved her
I'd say that the world began and ended where she was
O I'd swear that the Beautiful wept to see her naked loveliness

I'd want her thighs to put birds in my fingers
I'd want her belly to be as soft and warm as a sleeping kitten's
I'd want her sex to meet mine as flames kissing in a dream forest

And O I'd tell her that I loved her
I'd say that all the noblest things of earth and heaven
Were made more noble because she lived
And O I'd know that the prettiest angels knelt there
As she lay asleep in my arms

Gloire de Dijon

D. H. Lawrence

When she rises in the morning
I linger to watch her;
Spreads the bath-cloth underneath the window
And the sunbeams catch her
Glistening white on the shoulders,
While down her sides the mellow
Golden shadow glows as
She stoops to the sponge, and her swung breasts
Sway like full-blown yellow
Gloire de Dijon roses.

She drips herself with water, and the shoulders
Glisten as silver, they crumple up
Like wet and falling roses, and I listen
For the sluicing of their rain-dishevelled petals.
In the window full of sunlight
Concentrates her golden shadow
Fold on fold, until it glows as
Mellow as the glory roses.

Gulls Land and Cease To Be

John Ciardi

Spread back across the air, wings wide,
    legs out, the wind delicately
dumped in balance, the gulls ride
    down, down, hang, and exactly
touch, folding not quite at once
    into their gangling weight, but
taking one step, two, wings still askance,
    reluctantly, at last, shut,
    twitch one look around
    and are aground.

Composed upon Westminster Bridge, September 3, 1802

William Wordsworth

Earth has not anything to show more fair:
Dull would he be of soul who could pass by
A sight so touching in its majesty;
This city now doth, like a garment, wear
The beauty of the morning; silent, bare,
Ships, towers, domes, theatres, and temples lie
Open unto the fields, and to the sky;
All bright and glittering in the smokeless air.
Never did sun more beautifully steep
In his first splendour, valley, rock, or hill;
Ne'er saw I, never felt, a calm so deep!
The river glideth at his own sweet will:
Dear God! the very houses seem asleep;
And all that mighty heart is lying still!

Sonnet 76

William Shakespeare

Why is my verse so barren of new pride,
So far from variation or quick change?
Why with the time do I not glance aside
To new-found methods and to compounds strange?
Why write I still all one, ever the same,
And keep invention in a noted weed,
That every word doth almost tell my name,
Showing their birth and where they did proceed?
O, know, sweet love, I always write of you,
And you and love are still my argument;
So all my best is dressing old words new,
Spending again what is already spent:
    For as the sun is daily new and old,
    So is my love still telling what is told.

Success Is Counted Sweetest

Emily Dickinson

Success is counted sweetest
By those who ne'er succeed.
To comprehend a nectar
Requires sorest need.

Not one of all the purple Host
Who took the Flag today
Can tell the definition
So clear of Victory

As he defeated—dying—
On whose forbidden ear
The distant strains of triumph
Burst agonized and clear!

A Deep-Sworn Vow

William Butler Yeats

Others because you did not keep
That deep-sworn vow have been friends of mine;
Yet always when I look death in the face,
When I clamber to the heights of sleep,
Or when I grow excited with wine,
Suddenly I meet your face.

When You Are Old

William Butler Yeats

When you are old, and grey and full of sleep,
And nodding by the fire, take down this book,
And slowly read, and dream of the soft look
Your eyes had once, and of their shadows deep;

How many loved your moments of glad grace,
And loved your beauty with love false or true,
But one man loved the pilgrim soul in you,
And loved the sorrows of your changing face;

And bending down beside the glowing bars,
Murmur, a little sadly, how Love fled
And paced upon the mountains overhead
And hid his face amid a crowd of stars.

Touch

Thom Gunn

You are already
asleep. I lower
myself in next to
you, my skin slightly
numb with the restraint
of habits, the patina of
self, the black frost
of outsideness, so that even
unclothed it is
a resilient chilly
hardness, a superficially
malleable, dead
rubbery texture.

You are a mound
of bedclothes, where the cat
in sleep braces
its paws against your
calf through the blankets,
and kneads each paw in turn.

Meanwhile and slowly
I feel a is it
my own warmth surfacing or
the ferment of your whole
body that in darkness beneath
the cover is stealing
bit by bit to break
down that chill.

        You turn and
hold me tightly, do
you know who
I am or am I
your mother or
the nearest human being to
hold on to in a
dreamed pogrom.

What I, now loosened,
sink into is an old
big place, it is
there already, for
you are already
there, and the cat
got there before you, yet
it is hard to locate.
What is more, the place is
not found but seeps
from our touch in
continuous creation, dark
enclosing cocoon round
ourselves alone, dark
wide realm where we
walk with everyone.

from *Kaddish*

(For Naomi Ginsberg, 1894–1956)

Allen Ginsberg

. . . O Russian faced, woman on the grass, your long black
hair is crowned with flowers, the mandolin is on your knees—
    Communist beauty, sit here married in the summer among
daisies, promised happiness at hand—
    holy mother, now you smile on your love, your world
is born anew, children run naked in the field spotted with
dandelions,
    they eat in the plum tree grove at the end of the meadow
and find a cabin where a white-haired Negro teaches the mystery
of his rainbarrel—
    blessed daughter come to America, I long to hear your
voice again, remembering your mother's music, in the Song of
the Natural Front—
    O glorious muse that bore me from the womb, gave suck
first mystic life & taught me talk and music, from whose pained
head I first took Vision—
    Tortured and beaten in the skull—What mad hallucinations
of the damned that drive me out of my own skull to seek
Eternity till I find Peace for Thee, O Poetry—and for all
humankind call on the Origin.
    Death which is the mother of the universe!—Now wear
your nakedness forever, white flowers in your hair, your marriage
sealed behind the sky—no revolution might destroy that
maidenhood—
    O beautiful Garbo of my Karma . . .

Big Momma

Don L. Lee

finally retired   pensionless
from cleaning somebody else's house
she remained home to clean
the one she didn't own.

in her kitchen where we often talked
the *chicago tribune* served as a tablecloth
for the two cups of tomato soup that went
along with my weekly visit & talkingto.

she was in a seriously-funny mood
& from the get-go she was down, realdown:

> roaches around here are like
> letters on a newspaper
> or
> u gonta be a writer, hunh
> when u gona write me some writen
> or
> the way niggers act around here
> if talk cd kill we'd all be dead.

she's somewhat confused about all this blackness
but said that it's good when negroes start putting themselves
first and added: we've always shopped at the colored stores.
> & the way niggers cut each other up round
> here every weekend that whiteman don't
>   haveta
> worry bout no revolution specially when he's
> gonta haveta pay for it too, anyhow all he's
> gotta do is drop a truck load of dope out
>   there
> on 43rd st. & all the niggers & yr
>   revolutionaries
> be too busy getten high & then they'll turn
>   round
> and fight each other over who got the
>   mostest

we finished our soup and i moved to excuse myself,
as we walked to the front door she made a last comment:
>   now luther i knows you done changed a lots but if
>   you can think back, we never did eat too much pork
>   round here anyways, it was bad for the belly.
i shared her smile and agreed.

touching the snow lightly i headed for 43rd st.
at the corner i saw a brother crying   while
trying to hold up a lamp post,
thru his watery eyes i cd see big momma's words.

at sixty-eight
she moves freely, is often right
and when there is food
eats   joyously with her own
real teeth.

Harsh

The Distant Drum

Calvin C. Hernton

I am not a metaphor or symbol.
This you hear is not the wind in the trees,
Nor a cat being maimed in the street.
I am being maimed in the street.
It is I who weep, laugh, feel pain or joy,
Speak this because I exist.
This is my voice.
These words are my words,
My mouth speaks them,
My hand writes—
I am a poet.
It is my fist you hear
Beating against your ear.

Santa Claus

Howard Nemerov

Somewhere on his travels the strange Child
Picked up with this overstuffed confidence man,
Affection's inverted thief, who climbs at night
Down chimneys, into dreams, with this world's goods.
Bringing all the benevolence of money,
He teaches the innocent to want, thus keeps
Our fat world rolling. His prescribed costume,
White flannel beard, red belly of cotton waste,
Conceals the thinness of essential hunger,
An appetite that feeds on satisfaction;
Or, pregnant with possessions, he brings forth
Vanity and the void. His name itself
Is corrupted, and even Saint Nicholas, in his turn,
Gives off a faint and reminiscent stench,
The merest soupçon, of brimstone and the pit.

Now, at the season when the Child is born
To suffer for the world, suffer the world,
His bloated Other, jovial satellite
And sycophant, makes his appearance also
In a glitter of goodies, in a rock candy glare.
Played at better stores by bums, for money,
This annual savior of the economy
Speaks in the parable of the dollar sign:
Suffer the little children to come to Him.

At Easter, he's anonymous again,
Just one of the crowd lunching on Calvary.

Wisdom

Sara Teasdale

When I have ceased to break my wings
Against the faultiness of things,
And learned that compromises wait
Behind each hardly opened gate,
When I can look Life in the eyes,
Grown calm and very coldly wise,
Life will have given me the Truth,
And taken in exchange—my youth.

Africa's Plea

Roland Tombekai Dempster

I am not you—
but you will not
give me a chance,
will not let me be *me*.

"If I were you"—
but you know
I am not you,
yet you will not
let me be *me*.

You meddle, interfere
in my affairs
as if they were yours
and you were me.

You are unfair, unwise,
foolish to think
that I can be you,
talk, act
and think like you.

God made me *me*.
He made you *you*.
For God's sake
Let me be *me*.

London

William Blake

I wander thro' each charter'd street,
Near where the charter'd Thames does flow,
And mark in every face I meet
Marks of weakness, marks of woe.

In every cry of every Man,
In every Infant's cry of fear,
In every voice, in every ban,
The mind-forg'd manacles I hear.

How the Chimney-sweeper's cry
Every black'ning Church appalls;
And the hapless Soldier's sigh
Runs in blood down Palace walls.

But most thro' midnight streets I hear
How the youthful Harlot's curse
Blasts the new-born Infant's tear,
And blights with plagues the Marriage hearse.

Hello

Robert Creeley

With a quick
jump he caught
the edge of

her eye and
it tore, down,
ripping. She

shuddered,
with the unexpected
assault, but

to his vantage
he held by
what flesh was left.

Langston Hughes

Poet in Pal[o]

High School Prin[c]

Langston Hughes

Palo Alto High school authorities yesterday banned the use of the school auditorium for a speech by Negro Poet Langston Hughes.

Later in the day, however, the authorities announced they would reconsider their action.

A meeting at which Hughes is scheduled to be the feature speaker was set for next Wednesday evening. Sponsors of the speech are the Redwood City Council for Civic Unity and the Palo Alto branch of the National Association for the Advancement of Colored People.

Yesterday morning,

Impasse

Langston Hughes

I could tell you,
If I wanted to,
What makes me
What I am.

But I don't
Really want to—
And you don't
Give a damn.

A Bill to My Father

Edward Field

I am typing up bills for a firm to be sent to their clients.
It occurs to me that firms are sending bills to my father
Who has that way an identity I do not often realize.
He is a person who buys, owes, and pays,
Not papa like he is to me.
His creditors reproach him for not paying on time
With a bill marked "Please Remit."
I reproach him for never having shown his love for me
But only his disapproval.
He has a debt to me too
Although I have long since ceased asking him to come across;
He does not know how and so I do without it.
But in this impersonal world of business
He can be communicated with:
With absolute assurance of being paid
The boss writes "Send me my money"
And my father sends it.

Jealousy

Rupert Brooke

When I see you, who were so wise and cool,
Gazing with silly sickness on that fool
You've given your love to, your adoring hands
Touch his so intimately that each understands
I know, most hidden things; and when I know
Your holiest dreams yield to the stupid bow
Of his red lips, and that the empty grace
Of those strong legs and arms, that rosy face,
Has beaten your heart to such a flame of love,
That you have given him every touch and move,
Wrinkle and secret of you, all your life,
—Oh! then I know I'm waiting, lover-wife,
For the great time when love is at a close,
And all its fruit's to watch the thickening nose
And sweaty neck and dulling face and eye,
That are yours, and you, most surely, till you die!
Day after day you'll sit with him and note
The greasier tie, the dingy wrinkling coat;
As prettiness turns to pomp, and strength to fat,
And love, love, love to habit!

                And after that,
When all that's fine in man is at an end,
And you, that loved young life and clean, must tend
A foul sick fumbling dribbling body and old,
When his rare lips hang flabby and can't hold
Slobber, and you're enduring that worst thing,
Senility's queasy furtive love-making,
And searching those dear eyes for human meaning,
Propping the bald and helpless head, and cleaning
A scrap that life's flung by, and love's forgotten,—
Then you'll be tired; and passion dead and rotten;
And he'll be dirty, dirty!

              O lithe and free
And lightfoot, that the poor heart cries to see,
That's how I'll see your man and you!—

                  But you
—Oh, when *that* time comes, you'll be dirty too!

A Teacher

Reed Whittemore

He hated them all one by one but wanted to show them
What was Important and Vital and by God if
They thought they'd never have use for it he was
Sorry as hell for them, that's all, with their genteel
Mercantile Main Street Babbitt
Bourgeois-barbaric faces, they were beyond
Saving, clearly, quite out of reach, and so he
G-rrr
Got up every morning and g-rrr ate his breakfast
And g-rrr lumbered off to his eight o'clock
Gladly to teach.

Five Ways to Kill a Man

Edwin Brock

There are many cumbersome ways to kill a man:
you can make him carry a plank of wood
to the top of a hill and nail him to it. To do this
properly you require a crowd of people
wearing sandals, a cock that crows, a cloak
to dissect, a sponge, some vinegar and one
man to hammer the nails home.

Or you can take a length of steel,
shaped and chased in a traditional way,
and attempt to pierce the metal cage he wears.
But for this you need white horses,
English trees, men with bows and arrows,
at least two flags, a prince and a
castle to hold your banquet in.

Dispensing with nobility, you may, if the wind
allows, blow gas at him. But then you need
a mile of mud sliced through with ditches,
not to mention black boots, bomb craters,
more mud, a plague of rats, a dozen songs
and some round hats made of steel.

In an age of aeroplanes, you may fly
miles above your victim and dispose of him by
pressing one small switch. All you then
require is an ocean to separate you, two
systems of government, a nation's scientists,
several factories, a psychopath and
land that no one needs for several years.

These are, as I began, cumbersome ways
to kill a man. Simpler, direct, and much more neat
is to see that he is living somewhere in the middle
of the twentieth century, and leave him there.

Young worker in a cotton mill—North Carolina, 1908

The Golf Links Lie So Near the Mill

Sarah N. Cleghorn

The golf links lie so near the mill
    That almost every day
The laboring children can look out
    And see the men at play.

Discovery

Hilaire Belloc

Life is a long discovery, isn't it?
You only get your wisdom bit by bit.
If you have luck you find in early youth
How dangerous it is to tell the Truth;
And next you learn how dignity and peace
Are the ripe fruits of patient avarice.
You find that middle life goes racing past.
You find despair: and, at the very last,
You find as you are giving up the ghost
That those who loved you best despised you most.

True Love at Last

D. H. Lawrence

The handsome and self-absorbed young man
looked at the lovely and self-absorbed girl
and thrilled.

The lovely and self-absorbed girl
looked back at the handsome and self-absorbed young man
and thrilled.

And in that thrill he felt:
Her self-absorption is even as strong as mine.
I must see if I can't break through it
and absorb her in me.

And in that thrill she felt:
His self-absorption is even stronger than mine!
What fun, stronger than mine!
I must see if I can't absorb this Samson of self-absorption.

So they simply adored one another
and in the end they were both nervous wrecks, because
in self-absorption and self-interest they were equally matched.

In the Convalescent Hospital

Jean Pumphrey

We try to give the best patient
care available in our community.

That dandy,
82 years old,
he ought to be- dead,
ought to be poisoned,
like me,
but they won't let me be,
and you are a liar,
I don't feel brightly
like you say my dress is,
I grin a smile
bright as blood
or this dress,
this garbage bag
I'm wearing,
or these diamonds
ringing my fingers
like life preservers,
I hate him,
and her too,
and you,
he stole my cigarettes,
and I told her,
when she said she nearly died,
ha-ha, to go do it
for all of us,
like Christ!
and you are alive,
there on the other side,
peering at me in this cage
from your cage of flesh,
thinking you aren't dying,
that my life is death-talk,
but here they all love me,
they love me.

I Shall Not Care

Sara Teasdale

When I am dead and over me bright April
    Shakes out her rain-drenched hair,
Tho' you should lean above me broken-hearted,
    I shall not care.

I shall have peace, as leafy trees are peaceful
    When rain bends down the bough,
And I shall be more silent and cold-hearted
    Than you are now.

Tomorrow, and Tomorrow, and Tomorrow

William Shakespeare

Tomorrow, and tomorrow, and tomorrow,
Creeps in this petty pace from day to day,
To the last syllable of recorded time;
And all our yesterdays have lighted fools
Their way to dusty death. Out, out, brief candle!
Life's but a walking shadow, a poor player,
That struts and frets his hour upon the stage,
And then is heard no more, it is a tale
Told by an idiot, full of sound and fury,
Signifying nothing.

American Rhapsody (2)

Kenneth Fearing

First you bite your fingernails. And then you comb
    your hair again. And then you wait. And wait.
(They say, you know, that first you lie. And then you
    steal, they say. And then, they say, you kill.)

Then the doorbell rings. Then Peg drops in. And Bill.
    And Jane. And Doc.
And first you talk, and smoke, and hear the news and
    have a drink. Then you walk down the stairs.
And you dine, then, and go to a show after that,
    perhaps, and after that a night spot, and after
that come home again, and climb the stairs
    again, and again go to bed.

But first Peg argues, and Doc replies. First you dance
    the same dance and you drink the same drink
    you always drank before.
And the piano builds a roof of notes above the world·
And the trumpet weaves a dome of music through
    space. And the drum makes a ceiling over space
    and time and night.
And then the table-wit. And then the check. Then
    home again to bed.
But first, the stairs

And do you now, baby, as you climb the stairs, do
    you still feel as you felt back there?
Do you feel again as you felt this morning? And the
    night before? And the night before that?
(They say, you know, that first you hear voices. And
    then you have visions, they say. Then, they say,
    you kick and scream and rave.)
Or do you feel: What is one more night in a lifetime
    of nights?
What is one more death, or friendship, or divorce
    out of two, or three? Or four? Or five?
One more face among so many, many faces, one more
    life among so many million lives?

But first, baby, as you climb and count the stairs
    (and they total the same) did you, sometime or
    somewhere, have a different idea?
Is this, baby, what you were born to feel, and do, and be?

For Saundra

Nikki Giovanni

i wanted to write
a poem
that rhymes
but revolution doesn't lend
itself to be-bopping

then my neighbor
who thinks i hate
asked—do you ever write
tree poems—i like trees
so i thought
i'll write a beautiful green tree poem
peeked from my window
to check the image
noticed the school yard was covered
with asphalt
no green—no trees grow
in manhattan

then, well, i thought the sky
i'll do a big blue sky poem
but all the clouds have winged
low since no-Dick was elected

so i thought again
and it occurred to me
maybe i shouldn't write
at all
but clean my gun
and check my kerosene supply

perhaps these are not poetic
times
at all

Hour of Concern

Lindley Williams Hubbell

When Albert Einstein appeared
on television telling
of the destructiveness of the atom bomb
my countrymen were swept by hysteria

about Ingrid Bergman's baby
and everyone was telling dirty jokes
about Stromboli sandwiches
and Stromboli cocktails.

But when four nuclear physicists produced
scientific proof that the hydrogen bomb
could destroy all life on this planet
then my countrymen became really concerned

about a leopard that had escaped
from the zoo in Oklahoma City
and was wandering at liberty
in the adjacent woods.

New Approach Needed

Kingsley Amis

Should you revisit us,
Stay a little longer,
And get to know the place.
Experience hunger,
Madness, disease and war.
You heard about them, true,
The last time you came here;
It's different having them.
And what about a go
at love, marriage, children?
All good, but bringing some
Risk of remorse and pain
And fear of an odd sort:
A sort one should, again,
Feel, not just hear about,
To be qualified as
A human-race expert.
On local life, we trust
The resident witness,
Not the royal tourist.

People have suffered worse
And more durable wrongs
Than you did on that cross
(I know—you won't get me
Up on one of those things),
Without much prospect of
Ascending good as new
On the third day, without
'I die, but man shall live'
As a nice cheering thought.

So, next time, come off it,
And get some service in,
Jack, long before you start
To lay down the old law:
If you still want to then.
Tell your dad that from me.

Dear America

Robert Peterson

> We are humanitarians.—*Lyndon B. Johnson*
> No lie lives forever.—*Carlyle*

Dear America you worry me.
Our friendship (& that's all it ever was)
is shaky.

I don't trust you
or your Dreams
or your Destiny
any more.

No longer Gem of the Ocean,
no longer Land of the Free,
your house no more the Golden Door

Who are you to ask me to be a statistic
or a lizard? (No I won't shut up.)

Trying to hand my body over to Ministers
& Generals, throwing me out False Reports,

killing kids & calling it News.

I know an ugly mirage when I see one.
Your Power grunts in cannon, is dying
in smoke rings . . .

Don't tell me what is good for me,
I'll make up my own poor mind.
The Last Mile is a lonesome road,
go bomb a canoe.

Poem to a Nigger Cop

Bobb Hamilton

Hey there poleece
Black skin in blue mask
You really gonna uphold the law?
What you gonna do when you see
Your Mama
Running down 125th street with
A. t.v. set tied up in a bandana trying to catch the train to
Springfield Gardens?
You mean to tell me you gonna
Bang your own mother?
Bang! Bang!
I can see you now grinning
A big black no nuts nigger
On channel number 5
Your teeth rolling across the screen
Like undotted dice
Talking about how you "uphelt
De Law."
While Mr. Charlie sticks his white
Finger up your ass
And pins a little gold medal on your
Chest!
And then you'll bust out into soft shoe shuffle
While a background chorus sings
"God Bless America,"
With an Irish accent.

Mourn Not the Dead

Ralph Chaplin

Mourn not the dead that in the cool earth lie—
Dust unto dust—
The calm sweet earth that mothers all who die
As all men must;

Mourn not your captive comrades who must dwell—
Too strong to strive—
Each in his steel-bound coffin of a cell,
Buried alive;

But rather mourn the apathetic throng—
The cowed and the meek—
Who see the world's great anguish and its wrong
And dare not speak!

The Leaden-Eyed

Vachel Lindsay

Let not young souls be smothered out before
They do quaint deeds and fully flaunt their pride.
It is the world's one crime its babes grow dull,
Its poor are ox-like, limp and leaden-eyed.

Not that they starve, but starve so dreamlessly,
Not that they sow, but that they seldom reap,
No that they serve, but have no gods to serve,
Not that they die, but that they die like sheep.

American Primitive

William Jay Smith

Look at him there in his stovepipe hat,
His high-top shoes, and his handsome collar;
Only my Daddy could look like that,
And I love my Daddy like he loves his Dollar.

The screen door bangs, and it sounds so funny—
There he is in a shower of gold;
His pockets are stuffed with folding money,
His lips are blue, and his hands feel cold.

He hangs in the hall by his black cravat,
The ladies faint, and the children holler:
Only my Daddy could look like that,
And I love my Daddy like he loves his Dollar.

Mothers, Daughters

Shirley Kaufman

Through every night we hate,
preparing the next day's
war. She bangs the door.
Her face laps up my own
despair, the sour, brown eyes,
the heavy hair she won't
tie back. She's cruel,
as if my private meanness
found a way to punish us.

We gnaw at each other's
skulls. Give me what's mine.
I'd haul her back, choking
myself in her, herself
in me. There is a book
called *Poisons* on her shelf.
Her room stinks with incense,
animal turds, hamsters
she strokes like silk. They
exercise on the bathroom
floor, and two drop through
the furnace vent. The whole
house smells of the accident,
the hot skins, the small
flesh rotting. Six days
we turn the gas up then
to fry the dead. I'd fry
her head if I could until
she cried love, love me!

All she won't let me do.
Her stringy figure in
the windowed room shares
its thin bones with no one.
Only her shadow on the glass
waits like an older sister.
Now she stalks, leans forward,
concentrates merely on getting
from here to there. Her feet
are bare. I hear her breathe
where I can't get in. If I
break through to her, she will
drive nails into my tongue.

Daddy

Sylvia Plath

You do not do, you do not do
Any more, black shoe
In which I have lived like a foot
For thirty years, poor and white.
Barely daring to breathe or Achoo.

Daddy, I have had to kill you.
You died before I had time—
Marble-heavy, a bag full of God,
Ghastly statue with one grey toe
Big as a Frisco seal

And a head in the freakish Atlantic
Where it pours bean green over blue
In the waters off beautiful Nauset.
I used to pray to recover you.
Achu, du.

In the German tongue, in the Polish town
Scraped flat by the roller
Of wars, wars, wars.
But the name of the town is common.
My Polack friend

Says there are a dozen or two.
So I never could tell where you
Put your foot, your root,
I never could talk to you.
The tongue stuck in my jaw.

It stuck in a barb wire snare.
Ich, ich, ich, ich,
I could hardly speak.
I thought every German was you.
And the language obscene

An engine, an engine
Chuffing me off like a Jew.
A Jew to Dachau, Auschwitz, Belsen.
I began to talk like a Jew.
I think I may well be a Jew.

The snows of the Tyrol, the clear beer of Vienna
Are not very pure or true.
With my gypsy ancestress and my weird luck
And my Taroc pack and my Taroc pack
I may be a bit of a Jew.

I have always been scared of *you*,
With your Luftwafte, your gobbledygoo.
And your neat moustache
And your Aryan eye, bright blue.
Panzer-man, panzer-man, O *You*—

Not God but a swastika
So black no sky could squeak through.
Every woman adores a Fascist,
The boot in the face, the brute
Brute heart of a brute like you.

You stand at the blackboard, daddy,
In the picture I have of you,
A cleft in your chin instead of your foot
But no less a devil for that, no not
Any less the black man who

Bit my pretty red heart in two.
I was ten when they buried you.
At twenty I tried to die
And get back, back, back to you.
I thought even the bones would do.

But they pulled me out of the sack,
And they stuck me together with glue.
And then I knew what to do.
I made a model of you,
A man in black with a Meinkampf look

And a love of the rack and the screw.
And I said I do, I do.
So daddy, I'm finally through.
The black telephone's off at the root,
The voices just can't worm through.

If I've killed one man, I've killed *two*—
The vampire who said he was you
And drank my blood for a year,

Seven years, if you want to know.
Daddy, you can lie back now.

There's a stake in your fat black heart
And the villagers never liked you.
They are dancing and stamping on you.
They always *knew* it was you.
Daddy, daddy, you bastard, I'm through.

Light

Introduction to
Songs of Innocence

William Blake

Piping down the valleys wild,
Piping songs of pleasant glee,
On a cloud I saw a child,
And he, laughing, said to me:

"Pipe a song about a Lamb!"
So I piped with merry cheer.
"Piper, pipe that song again";
So I piped: he wept to hear.

"Drop thy pipe, thy happy pipe;
Sing thy songs of happy cheer":
So I sang the same again,
While he wept with joy to hear.

"Piper, sit thee down, and write
In a book, that all may read."
So he vanished from my sight,
And I plucked a hollow reed,

And I made a rural pen,
And I stained the water clear,
And I wrote my happy songs
Every child may joy to hear.

The Perforated Spirit

Morris Bishop

The fellows up in Personnel,
    They have a set of cards on me.
The sprinkled perforations tell
    My individuality.

And what am I? I am a chart
    Upon the cards of IBM;
The secret places of the heart
    Have little secrecy for them.

It matters not how I may prate,
    They punch with punishments my scroll.
The files are masters of my fate,
    They are the captains of my soul.

Monday my brain began to buzz;
    I was in agony all night.
I found out what the trouble was:
    They had my paper clip too tight.

An Elegy
on the Death of a Mad Dog

Oliver Goldsmith

Good people all, of every sort,
  Give ear unto my song;
And if you find it wondrous short,—
  It cannot hold you long.

In Islington there was a man,
  Of whom the world might say,
That still a godly race he ran,—
  Whene'er he went to pray.

A kind and gentle heart he had,
  To comfort friends and foes;
The naked every day he clad,—
  When he put on his clothes.

And in that town a dog was found,
  As many dogs there be,
Both mongrel, puppy, whelp, and hound,
  And curs of low degree.

This dog and man at first were friends;
  But when a pique began,
The dog, to gain some private ends,
  Went mad, and a bit the man.

Around from all the neighboring streets
  The wondering neighbors ran,
And swore the dog had lost his wits,
  To bite so good a man.

The wound it seemed both sore and sad
  To every Christian eye;
And while they swore the dog was mad,
  They swore the man would die.

But soon a wonder came to light,
  That showed the rogues they lied;
The man recovered of the bite,
  The dog it was that died.

The Naming of Cats

T. S. Eliot

The Naming of Cats is a difficult matter,
    It isn't just one of your holiday games;
You may think at first I'm mad as a hatter
When I tell you, a cat must have THREE DIFFER-
      ENT NAMES.
First of all, there's the name that the family use
      daily,
    Such as Peter, Augustus, Alonzo or James,
Such as Victor or Jonathan, George or Bill
      Bailey—
    All of them sensible everyday names.
There are fancier names if you think they sound
      sweeter,
    Some for the gentlemen, some for the
      dames;
Such as Plato, Admetus, Electra, Demeter—
    But all of them sensible everyday names.
But I tell you, a cat needs a name that's par-
      ticular,
    A name that's peculiar, and more dignified,
Else how can he keep up his tail perpen-
      dicular,
    Or spread out his whiskers, or cherish his
      pride?
Of names of this kind, I can give you a quorum,
    Such as Munkustrap, Quaxo, or Coricopat
Such as Bombalurina, or else Jellylorum—
    Names that never belong to more than one
      cat.
But above and beyond there's still one name left
      over,
    And that is the name that you never will
      guess;
The name that no human research can dis-
      cover—
    But THE CAT HIMSELF KNOWS, and will never
      confess.
When you notice a cat in profound medita-
      tion,
    The reason, I tell you, is always the same:
His mind is engaged in a rapt contemplation

Of the thought, of the thought, of the thought
of his name:
His ineffable effable
Effanineffable
Deep and inscrutable singular Name.

The Story of My Life

Hollis Summers

My mother, moving among improving books
And P.T.A. sylphs, tried to change her looks.
Influenced by whom she saw and what she read,
She dieted.

My father was influenced by who saw him
And what they said. He moved as a paradigm
Before mirrors and community eyes, a citizen
Clean shaven.

My father, dapperly established, strove
For the status quo. He said, if Jove
Had willed *He* would have made my mother thin
As a water moccasin.

My mother said that if the Lord had wished
My father to be shaved and pressed and polished,
He would have made him, with an Indian's head,
In wrinkleless worsted.

I listened to their talk and disapproved.
Now, decades later, I have moved
While watching my weight, beyond their cavilling,
Carefully shaving.

Grim Fairy Tale

Lionel Wiggam

I am the princess who kissed a frog
Who never changed to a charming prince.
Born a frog, he stayed a frog
Whose intimate sounds make a princess wince,
Who mocked her wistful stabs at culture,
Swilled like a shark, stuffed like a vulture,
Damned her beauty marks as moles,
Left paper floating in the bowls.

And wearied the princess who never heard
From the liverish lips an intuitive word,
Fouling her own fastidious nature
To dwell with such a sickening creature
Who banished her friends, bullied her brother,
Drove from the grounds her poor old mother,
Turned the house to a downright bog
And turned the princess into a frog.

The Frog Prince
A Speculation on Grimm's Fairy Tale

Robert Pack

Imagine the princess's surprise!
Who would have thought a frog's cold frame
Could hold the sweet and gentle body
Of a prince? How can I name
The joy she must have felt to learn
His transformation was the wonder
Of her touch—that she too, in
Her way, had been transformed under
Those clean sheets? Such powers were
Like nothing she had ever read.
And in the morning when the mother
Came and saw them there in bed,
Heard how a frog became a prince;
What was it that her mother said?

For Anne Gregory

William Butler Yeats

"Never shall a young man
Thrown into despair
By those great honey-coloured
Ramparts at your ear,
Love you for yourself alone
And not your yellow hair."

"But I can get a hair-dye
And set such colour there,
Brown, or black, or carrot,
That young men in despair
May love me for myself alone
And not my yellow hair."

"I heard an old religious man
But yesternight declare
That he had found a text to prove
That only God, my dear,
Could love you for yourself alone
And not your yellow hair."

Jabberwocky

Lewis Carroll

'Twas brillig, and the slithy toves
    Did gyre and gimble in the wabe:
All mimsy were the borogoves,
    And the mome raths outgrabe.

"Beware the Jabberwock, my son!
    The jaws that bite, the claws that catch!
Beware the Jubjub bird, and shun
    The frumious Bandersnatch!"

He took his vorpal sword in hand:
    Long time the manxome foe he sought—
So rested he by the Tumtum tree,
    And stood awhile in thought.

And, as in uffish thought he stood,
    The Jabberwock, with eyes of flame,
Came whiffling through the tulgey wood,
    And burbled as it came!

One, two! One, two! And through and through
    The vorpal blade went snicker-snack!
He left it dead, and with its head
    He went galumphing back.

"And hast thou slain the Jabberwock?
    Come to my arms, my beamish boy!
O frabjous day! Callooh! Callay!"
    He chortled in his joy.

'Twas brillig, and the slithy toves
    Did gyre and gimble in the wabe:
All mimsy were the borogoves,
    And the mome raths outgrabe.

Song of the Open Road

Ogden Nash

I think that I shall never see
A billboard lovely as a tree.
Perhaps, unless the billboards fall,
I'll never see a tree at all.

Dr. Fatt, Instructor

Donald Hall

And why does *Fatt* teach English? Why, because
A law school felt he could not learn the laws.
He waddles brilliantly from class to class,
Smiling at everyone, and at the grass.
"*Hamlet*," he tells his students, "you will find,
Concerns a man who can't make up his mind.
The Tempest? . . . It's the one with Ariel.
Are there more questions now?" But one can tell
That all his will, brains, and imagination
Are concentrated on a higher station:
He wants to be in the Administration.
Sometimes at parties he observes the Dean;
He giggles, coughs, and turns aquamarine.
Yet some day we will hear of "Dr. *Fatt*,
Vice-President in Charge of This or That."
I heard the Dean observe, at tea and cakes,
Face stuffed and sneering, "*Fatt* has what it takes."

Sometime During Eternity

Lawrence Ferlinghetti

Sometime during eternity
                    some guys show up
and one of them
                    who shows up real late
                                    is a kind of carpenter
from some square-type place
                            like Galilee
    and he starts wailing
                        and claiming he is hip
to who made heaven
                    and earth
                            and that the cat
    who really laid it on us
                        is his Dad

And moreover
    he adds
            It's all writ down
                        on some scroll-type parchments
which some henchmen
                leave lying around the Dead Sea somewheres
    a long time ago
                    and which you won't even find
for a coupla thousand years or so
                            or at least for
    nineteen hundred and fortyseven
                            of them
                    to be exact
                        and even then
nobody really believes them
                    or me
                        for that matter

You're hot
            they tell him
And they cool him
They stretch him on the Tree to cool
    And everybody after that
                        is always making models
            of this Tree
                    with Him hung up

and always crooning His name
                    and calling Him to come down
          and sit in
                on their combo
     as if he is *the* king cat
                who's got to blow
  or they can't quite make it
Only he don't come down
                from His Tree

Him just hang there
             on His Tree
                    looking real Petered out
          and real cool
                   and also
    according to a roundup
                of late world news
from the usual unreliable sources
                real dead

The Dover Bitch:
A Criticism of Life

(For Andrews Wanning)

Anthony Hecht

So there stood Matthew Arnold and this girl
With the cliffs of England crumbling away behind them,
And he said to her, "Try to be true to me,
And I'll do the same for you, for things are bad
All over, etc., etc.,"
Well now, I knew this girl. It's true she had read
Sophocles in a fairly good translation
And caught that bitter allusion to the sea,
But all the time he was talking she had in mind
The notion of what his whiskers would feel like
On the back of her neck. She told me later on
That after a while she got to looking out
At the lights across the channel, and really felt sad,
Thinking of all the wine and enormous beds
And blandishments in French and the perfumes.
And then she got really angry. To have been brought
All the way down from London, and then be addressed
As a sort of mournful cosmic last resort
Is really tough on a girl, and she was pretty.
Anyway, she watched him pace the room
And finger his watch-chain and seem to sweat a bit,
And then she said one or two unprintable things.
But you mustn't judge her by that. What I mean to say is,
She's really all right. I still see her once in a while
And she always treats me right. We have a drink
And I give her a good time, and perhaps it's a year
Before I see her again, but there she is.
Running to fat, but dependable as they come.
And sometimes I bring her a bottle of Nuit d'Amour.

President Langton

Daniel J. Langton

There will be no slogans, no mottoes,
just a quiet sweetness, limned with modesty.

Certain conundrums will have to be answered;
there is the matter of the raincoat at Abercrombie & Fitch,
the disastrous affair of Miss A. in the provincial city of P.,
my army records will have disappeared.

Some inner glow will soothe the populace,
they will notice I do not drink,
preen about my wit
and send me to foreign capitals
where I always speak the native's tongue.

I will translate Mao,
Mao will translate me;
I will beat Bobby Fisher at swimming
And Mark Spitz at chess;
I will not pass good laws
but I will strangle bad ones;
my wife will get to meet Brando
and Dylan's kids will play on the lawn;
each Christmas I will dispatch pardons
to obscure dealers in Texas,
I will buy my clothes off the rack
and say good-bye gently.

I will be missed.

Second Fig

Edna St. Vincent Millay

Safe upon the solid rock the ugly houses stand:
Come and see my shining palace built upon the sand!

American Gothic

To Satch[1]

Samuel Allen (Paul Vesey)

Sometimes I feel like I will never stop
Just go on forever
Til one fine mornin'
I'm gonna reach up and grab me a handfulla stars
Swing out my long lean leg
And whip three hot strikes burnin' down the heavens
And look over at God and say
How about that!

[1]Leroy "Satchell" Paige was the famous black baseball pitcher whose career stretched into five decades.

Underwear

Lawrence Ferlinghetti

I didn't get much sleep last night
thinking about underwear
Have you ever stopped to consider
underwear in the abstract
When you really dig into it
some shocking problems are raised
Underwear is something
we all have to deal with
Everyone wears
some kind of underwear
Even Indians
wear underwear
Even Cubans
wear underwear
The Pope wears underwear I hope
Underwear is worn by Negroes
The Governor of Louisiana
wears underwear
I saw him on TV
He must have had tight underwear
He squirmed a lot
Underwear can really get you in a bind
Negroes often wear
white underwear
which may lead to trouble
You have seen the underwear ads
for men and women
so alike but so different
Women's underwear holds things up
Men's underwear holds things down
Underwear is one thing
men and women have in common
Underwear is all we have between us
You have seen the three-color pictures
with crotches encircled
to show the areas of extra strength
and three-way stretch
promising full freedom of action
Don't be deceived
It's all based on the two-party system
which doesn't allow much freedom of choice

the way things are set up
America in its Underwear
struggles thru the night
Underwear controls everything in the end
Take foundation garments for instance
They are really fascist forms
of underground government
making people believe
something but the truth
telling you what you can or can't do
Did you ever try to get around a girdle
Perhaps Non-Violent Action
is the only answer
Did Gandhi wear a girdle?
Did Lady Macbeth wear a girdle
Was that why Macbeth murdered sleep?
And that spot she was always rubbing—
Was it really in her underwear?
Modern anglosaxon ladies
must have huge guilt complexes
always washing and washing and washing
Out damned spot—rub don't blot—
Underwear with spots very suspicious
Underwear with bulges very shocking
Underwear on clothesline a great flag of freedom
Someone has escaped his Underwear
May be naked somewhere
Help!
But don't worry
everybody's still hung up in it
There won't be no real revolution
And poetry still the underwear of the soul
And underwear still covering
a multitude of faults
in the geological sense—
strange sedimentary stones, inscrutable cracks!
And that only the beginning
For does not the body stay alive
after death
and still need its underwear
or outgrow it
some organs said to reach full maturity
only after the head stops holding them back?
If I were you I'd keep aside
an oversize pair of winter underwear
Do not go naked into that good night

and in the meantime
keep calm and warm and dry
No use stirring ourselves up prematurely
'over Nothing'
Move forward with dignity
hand in vest
Don't get emotional
And death shall have no dominion
There's plenty of time my darling
Are we not still young and easy
Don't shout

The Purist

Ogden Nash

I give you now Professor Twist,
A conscientious scientist.
Trustees exclaimed, "He never bungles!"
And sent him off to distant jungles.
Camped on a tropic riverside,
One day he missed his loving bride.
She had, the guide informed him later,
Been eaten by an alligator.
Professor Twist could not but smile.
"You mean," he said, "a crocodile."

Telephone Conversation

Wole Soyinka

The price seemed reasonable, location
Indifferent. The landlady swore she lived
Off premises. Nothing remained
But self-confession. "Madam," I warned,
"I hate a wasted journey—I am African."
Silence. Silenced transmission of
Pressurized good-breeding. Voice, when it came,
Lipstick coated, long gold-rolled
Cigarette-holder pipped. Caught I was, foully.
"HOW DARK?" . . . I had not misheard . . . "ARE YOU LIGHT
OR VERY DARK?" Button B. Button A. Stench
Of rancid breath of public hide-and-speak.
Red booth. Red pillar-box. Red double-tiered
Omnibus squelching tar. It was real! Shamed
By ill-mannered silence, surrender
Pushed dumbfoundment to beg simplification.
Considerate she was, varying the emphasis—
"ARE YOU DARK? OR VERY LIGHT?" Revelation came.
"You mean—like plain or milk chocolate?"
Her assent was clinical, crushing in its light
Impersonality. Rapidly, wave-length adjusted,
I chose. "West African sepia"—and as afterthought,
"Down in my passport." Silence for spectroscopic
Flight of fancy, till truthfulness clanged her accent
Head of the mouthpiece. "WHAT'S THAT?" conceding
"DON'T KNOW WHAT THAT IS." "Like brunette."
"THAT'S DARK, ISN'T IT?" "Not altogether.
Facially, I am brunette, but madam, you should see
The rest of me. Palm of hand, soles of my feet
Are a peroxide blonde. Friction, caused—
Foolishly, madam—by sitting down, has turned
My bottom raven black—One moment madam!"—sensing
Her receiver rearing on the thunderclap
About my ears—"Madam," I pleaded, "wouldn't you rather
See for yourself?"

The Bride of Frankenstein

Edward Field

The Baron has decided to mate the monster,
to breed him perhaps,
in the interests of pure science, his only god.

So he goes up into his laboratory
which he has built in the tower of the castle
to be as near the interplanetary forces as possible,
and puts together the prettiest monster-woman you ever saw
with a body like a pin-up girl
and hardly any stitching at all
where he sewed on the head of a raped and murdered beauty queen.

He sets his liquids burping, and coils blinking and buzzing,
and waits for an electric storm to send through the equipment
the spark vital for life.
The storm breaks over the castle
and the equipment really goes crazy
like a kitchen full of modern appliances
as the lightning juice starts oozing right into that pretty corpse.

He goes to get the monster
so he will be right there when she opens her eyes,
for she might fall in love with the first thing she sees as ducklings do.
That monster is already straining at his chains and slurping,
ready to go right to it:
He has been well prepared for coupling
by his pinching leering keeper who's been saying for weeks,
"Ya gonna get a little nookie, kid,"
or "How do you go for some poontag, baby?"
All the evil in him is focused on this one thing now
as he is led into her very presence.

She awakens slowly,
she bats her eyes,
she gets up out of the equipment,
and finally she stands in all her seamed glory,
a monster princess with a hairdo like a fright-wig,
lightning flashing in the background
like a halo and a wedding veil,
like a photographer snapping pictures of great moments.

She stands and stares with her electric eyes,
beginning to understand that in this life too
she was just another body to be raped.
The monster is ready to go:
He roars with joy at the sight of her,
so they let him loose and he goes right for those knockers.
And she starts screaming to break your heart
and you realize that she was just born:
In spite of her big tits she was just a baby.

But her instincts are right—
rather death than that green slobber:
She jumps off the parapet.
And then the monster's sex drive goes wild.
Thwarted, it turns to violence, demonstrating sublimation crudely;
and he wrecks the lab, those burping acids and buzzing coils,
overturning the control panel so the equipment goes off like a bomb,
the stone castle crumbles and crashes in the storm
destroying them all . . . perhaps.

Perhaps somehow the Baron got out of that wreckage of his dreams
with his evil intact, if not his good looks,
and more wicked than ever went on with his thrilling career.

And perhaps even the monster lived
to roam the earth, his desire still ungratified,
and lovers out walking in shadowy and deserted places
will see his shape loom up over them, their doom—
and children sleeping in their beds
will wake up in the dark night screaming
as his hideous body grabs them.

The Plot to Assassinate the Chase Manhattan Bank

Carl Larsen

To assassinate the Chase Manhattan Bank
Is not as easy as you'd think.
I walked in, see, and yelled "Kings-X!"
and saw what looked like great machines
come rumbling to a halt, and I thought,
fine—I'm halfway home. Then God rose from
the Office of the President,
a little miffed, I think, and said,
"What's on your mind?"
"I came up from the Coast," I said,
"to blow this pad to—if you will
excuse my pun—to Kingdom Come."
"You can't do that, my Son," he said,
and that's how I knew he was God,
although he looked a great deal
like John Wayne. "You wouldn't want,"
he said, "to do away with this—"
and from each teller's cage, a flock
of rainbow doves flew up, and settled
near the roof. "Put down your bomb,
let's have a talk," he said, and smiled.
I laid aside the bomb and followed him
into his office, and sat down.
"The Proletariat demands," I said,
"You cease this madness"; And he
smiled again. I saw he had a golden tooth.
"Some for the glories of this world,"
God said, then showed a picture of his family,
and then his house, a nice split-level
place up in the Bronx. His wife,
a pleasant-looking woman,
had inscribed it: "Love, In God We Trust."
He wiped away the tears that gathered
in the corners of his steely eyes,
choked back a sob, and called The Fuzz.
Inside a minute, forty cops popped from
the walls and drawers, came running from
the vault where God kept love, and
clamped the irons around my feet.

"Now Jean Valjean," God shouted,
gaining his composure, "now you'll
face the rack!" I pleaded it was all
a joke. I said I'd be a good li'l boy
and stay home playing with my spiders
if he'd let me go. But his bit was not
forgiveness, and they locked me in
a dungeon full of nasty things he had
discarded, like the stars,
and sea-foam, and the earth.

The Rebel

Mari E. Evans

When I
die
I'm sure
I will have a
Big Funeral . . .
Curiosity
seekers . . .
coming to see
if I
am really
Dead . . .
or just
trying to make
Trouble. . . .

The Artist

William Carlos Williams

Mr. T
        bareheaded
             in a soiled undershirt
his hair standing out
        on all sides
             stood on his toes
heels together
        arms gracefully
             for the moment
curled about his head.
        Then he whirled about
             bounded
into the air
        and with an *entrechat*
             perfectly achieved
completed the figure.
        My mother
             taken by surprise
where she sat
        in her invalid's chair
             was left speechless.
Bravo! she cried at last
        and clapped her hands.
             The man's wife
came from the kitchen:
        What goes on here? she said.
             But the show was over.

Horror Movie

Howard Moss

Dr. Unlikely, we love you so.
You who made the double-headed rabbits grow
From a single hare. Mutation's friend,
Who could have prophecied the end
When the Spider Woman deftly snared the fly
And the monsters, strangled in a monstrous kiss
And somebody hissed, "You'll hang for this!"?

Dear Dracula, sleeping on your native soil,
(Any other kind makes him spoil),
How we clapped when you broke the French door down
And surprised the bride in the overwrought bed.
Perfectly dressed for lunar research,
Your evening cape added much,
Though the bride, inexplicably dressed in furs,
Was a study in jaded jugulars.

Poor, tortured Leopard Man, you changed your spots
In the debauched village of the Pin-Head Tots;
How we wrung our hands, how we wept
When the eighteenth murder proved inept,
And, caught in the Phosphorous Cave of Sea,
Dangling the last of synthetic flesh,
You said, "There's something wrong with me."

The Wolf Man knew when he prowled at dawn,
Beginnings spin a web where endings spawn.
The bat who lived on shaving cream,
A household pet of Dr. Dream,
Unfortunately, maddened by the bedlam,
Turned on the Doc, bit the hand that fed him.

And you, Dr. X, who killed by moonlight,
We loved your scream in the laboratory
When the panel slid and the night was starry
And you threw the inventor in the crocodile pit
(An obscure point: Did he deserve it?)
And you took the gold to Transylvania
Where no one guessed how insane you were.

We thank you for the moral and the mood,
Dear Dr. Cliché, Nurse Platitude.
When we meet again by the Overturned Grave,
Near the Sunken City of the Twisted Mind,
(In *The Son of the Son of Frankenstein*),
Make the blood flow, make the motive muddy:
There's a little death in every body.

The Origin Of Baseball

Kenneth Patchen

Someone had been walking in and out
Of the world without coming
To much decision about anything.
The sun seemed too hot most of the time.
There weren't enough birds around
And the hills had a silly look
When he got on top of one.
The girls in heaven, however, thought
Nothing of asking to see his watch
Like you would want someone to tell
A joke—'Time,' they'd say, 'what's
That mean—time?' laughing with the edges
Of their white mouths, like a flutter of paper
In a madhouse. And he'd stumble over
General Sherman or Elizabeth B.
Browning, muttering, 'Can't you keep
Your big wings out of the aisle?' But down
Again, there'd be millions of people without
Enough to eat and men with guns just
Standing there shooting each other.

So he wanted to throw something
And he picked up a baseball.

An Easy Decision

Kenneth Patchen

I had finished my dinner
Gone for a walk
It was fine
Out and I started whistling.

It wasn't long before

I met a
Man and his wife riding on
A pony with seven
Kids running along beside them

I said hello and

Went on
Pretty soon I met another
Couple
This time with nineteen
Kids and all of them
Riding on
A big smiling hippopotamus

I invited them home

she being Brand

e. e. cummings

she being Brand

—new;and you
know consequently a
little stiff i was
careful of her and (having

thoroughly oiled the universal
joint tested my gas felt of
her radiator made sure her springs were O.

K.)i went right to it flooded-the-carburetor cranked her

up,slipped the
clutch(and then somehow got into reverse she
kicked what
the hell)next
minute i was back in neutral tried and

again slo-wly;bare,ly nudg.   ing (my

lev-er Right–
oh and her gears being in
A 1 shape passed
from low through
second-in-to-high like
greased lightning just as we turned the corner of Divinity

avenue i touched the accelerator and give

her the juice,good

                    it
was the first ride and believe i we was
happy to see how nice she acted right up to
the last minute coming back down by the Public
Gardens i slammed on
the

internalexpanding
&
externalcontracting
brakes Bothatonce and

brought allofher tremB
-ling
to a:dead.

stand-
;Still)

Love Song

Dorothy Parker

My own dear love, he is strong and bold
    And he cares not what comes after.
His words ring sweet as a chime of gold,
    And his eyes are lit with laughter.
He is jubilant as a flag unfurled—
    Oh, a girl, she'd not forget him.
My own dear love, he is all my world—
    And I wish I'd never met him.

My love, he's mad, and my love, he's fleet,
    And a wild young wood-thing bore him!
The ways are fair to his roaming feet,
    And the skies are sunlit for him.
As sharply sweet to my heart he seems
    As the fragrance of acacia.
My own dear love, he is all my dreams—
    And I wish he were in Asia.

My love runs by like a day in June,
    And he makes no friends of sorrows.
He'll tread his galloping rigadoon
    In the pathway of the morrows.
He'll live his days where the sunbeams start,
    Nor could storm or wind uproot him.
My own dear love, he is all my heart—
    And I wish somebody'd shoot him.

A Sane Revolution

D. H. Lawrence

If you make a revolution, make it for fun,
don't make it in ghastly seriousness,
don't do it in deadly earnest,
do it for fun.

Don't do it because you hate people,
do it just to spit in their eye.

Don't do it for the money,
do it and be damned to the money.

Don't do it for equality,
do it because we've got too much equality
and it would be fun to upset the apple-cart
and see which way the apples would go a-rolling.

Don't do it for the working classes.
Do it so that we can all of us be little aristocracies on our own
and kick our heels like jolly escaped asses.

Don't do it, anyhow, for international Labour.
Labour is the one thing a man has had too much of.
Let's abolish labour, let's have done with labouring!
Work can be fun, and men can enjoy it; then it's not labour.
Let's have it so! Let's make a revolution for fun!

God and Man

Samuel Hazo

After casting the first act, checking sections
of scenery and mastering his rage
because the female lead blundered on page
one, he left the actors to themselves on stage
without a script and fretting for directions.

God Is Mr. Big, Real Big

Interpretations of the Ten Commandments (Exodus 20:3-17)

Carl F. Burke

1. *You shall have no other gods before me. . . .*
   Means God's the leader—nobody, but nobody, man, gets in the way. This is the top. He is Mr. Big, real big.

2. *You shall not make for yourself a graven image. . . .*
   This means no making things that look like God in the craftshop at the settlement house. No worship things like rabbits' foots and lucky dice and, damn it, dolls.

3. *You shall not take the name of the Lord your God in vain. . . .*
   It means knock off the swearing, or you better watch out.

4. *Observe the Sabbath day, to keep it holy. . . .*
   a. It means going to church on Sunday and listen to people who don't know much about what they are talking about.
   b. Keeping holy means no snatching purses on Sunday.
   c. Means: Taking a rest on Sunday—like my old man not feeling bad 'cause he can't find a job and loafing around at the gin mill.

5. *Honor your father and your mother. . . .*
   a. It means no calling your father a wino or your mother the old lady, even if they are.
   b. It means to love your mother, even if she hollers at you, and try to understand she is tired from working all day. It means to try to love your father, even if you don't know him or where he is.
   c. Maybe the others are OK, but this one is a real gasser—honor my father and mother—to hell with that, man!

6. *You shall not kill. . . .*
   a. No holding up people with switch blades.
   b. No playing chicken in the freight yards.
   c. No real rough fighting.

7. *Neither shall you commit adultery. . . .*
   a. No messing around with girls in the park.
   b. No whoring around.

8. *Neither shall you steal. . . .*
   That's it, don't need to say more.
   Why not? Everybody does it.

9. *Neither shall you bear false witness. . . .*
   No telling lies to the cops or in court, no matter how
   many breaks they say they'll give you.

10. *Neither shall you covet. . . .*
    a. Stop being so sorry for yourself and always wanting
       something you ain't got. (Feeling sorry only takes up time
       when you could be shining shoes to earn money to get
       the things you covet.)
    b. You ain't supposed to do it—but it's not so bad if it
       makes you try hard to get something you ain't got—
       if you don't get it by shoplifting.

Heavy

When The Ripe Fruit Falls

D. H. Lawrence

When the ripe fruit falls
its sweetness distils and trickles away into the veins of the earth.

When fulfilled people die
the essential oil of their experience enters
the veins of living space, and adds a glisten
to the atom, to the body of immortal chaos.

For space is alive
and it stirs like a swan
whose feathers glisten
silky with oil of distilled experience.

To Look at Any Thing

John Moffitt

To look at any thing,
If you would know that thing,
You must look at it long:
To look at this green and say
"I have seen spring in these
Woods," will not do—you must
Be the thing you see:
You must be the dark snakes of
Stems and ferny plumes of leaves,
You must enter in
To the small silences between
The leaves,
You must take your time
And touch the very peace
They issue from.

Hurt Hawks

Robinson Jeffers

I

The broken pillar of the wing jags from the clotted shoulder,
The wing trails like a banner in defeat,
No more to use the sky forever but live with famine
And pain a few days: cat nor coyote
Will shorten the week of waiting for death, there is game without
  talons.
He stands under the oak-bush and waits
The lame feet of salvation; at night he remembers freedom
And flies in a dream, the dawns ruin it.
He is strong and pain is worse to the strong, incapacity is worse.
The curs of the day come and torment him
At distance, no one but death the redeemer will humble that head,
The intrepid readiness, the terrible eyes.
The wild God of the world is sometimes merciful to those
That ask mercy, not often to the arrogant.
You do not know him, you communal people, or you have forgotten
  him;
Intemperate and savage, the hawk remembers him;
Beautiful and wild, the hawks, and men that are dying, remember him.

II

I'd sooner, except the penalties, kill a man than a hawk, but the great
  redtail
Had nothing left but unable misery
From the bone too shattered for mending, the wing that trailed under
  his talons when he moved.
We had fed him six weeks, I gave him freedom,
He wandered over the foreland hill and returned in the evening,
  asking for death,
Not like a beggar, still eyed with the old
Implacable arrogance. I gave him the lead gift in the twilight. What
  fell was relaxed,
Owl-downy, soft feminine feathers; but what
Soared: the fierce rush: the night-herons by the flooded river cried
  fear at its rising
Before it was quite unsheathed from reality.

I Think I Could Turn and Live with Animals

Walt Whitman

I think I could turn and live with animals, they are so placid
   and self-contained;
I stand and look at them long and long.
They do not sweat and whine about their condition;
They do not lie awake in the dark and weep for their sins;
They do not make me sick discussing their duty to God;
Not one is dissatisfied—not one is demented with the mania
   of owning things;
Not one kneels to another, nor to his kind that lived thousands
   of years ago;
Not one is respectable or industrious over the whole earth.

it is so long since my heart has been with yours

e. e. cummings

it is so long since my heart has been with yours

shut by our mingling arms through
a darkness where new lights begin and
increase,
since your mind has walked into
my kiss as a stranger
into the streets and colours of a town—

that i have perhaps forgotten
how, always (from
these hurrying crudities
of blood and flesh) Love
coins His most gradual gesture,

and whittles life to eternity

—after which our separating selves become museums
filled with skilfully stuffed memories

The Horse Chestnut Tree

Richard Eberhart

Boys in sporadic but tenacious droves
Come with sticks, as certainly as Autumn,
To assault the great horse chestnut tree.

There is a law governs their lawlessness.
Desire is in them for a shining amulet
And the best are those that are highest up.

They will not pick them easily from the ground.
With shrill arms they fling to the higher branches,
To hurry the work of nature for their pleasure.

I have seen them trooping down the street
Their pockets stuffed with chestnuts shucked, unshucked.
It is only evening keeps them from their wish.

Sometimes I run out in a kind of rage
To chase the boys away: I catch an arm,
Maybe, and laugh to think of being the lawgiver.

I was once such a young sprout myself
And fingered in my pocket the prize and trophy.
But still I moralize upon the day

And see that we, outlaws on God's property,
Fling out imagination beyond the skies,
Wishing a tangible good from the unknown.

And likewise death will drive us from the scene
With the great flowering world unbroken yet,
Which we held in idea, a little handful.

The End of the World

Archibald MacLeish

Quite unexpectedly as Vasserot
The armless ambidextrian was lighting
A match between his great and second toe
And Ralph the lion was engaged in biting
The neck of Madame Sossman while the drum
Pointed, and Teeny was about to cough
In waltz-time swinging Jocko by the thumb—
Quite unexpectedly the top blew off.

And there, there overhead, there, there, hung over
Those thousands of white faces, those dazed eyes,
There in the starless dark the poise, the hover,
There with vast wings across the canceled skies,
There in the sudden blackness, the black pall
Of nothing, nothing, nothing—nothing at all.

"Truly we can only allow our paintings to speak"

Vincent van Gogh

Jean Pumphrey

Vincent van Gogh
what must you have seen
to paint green faces
in a green world,
to make them flesh,
wheat fields
reflecting agony,
violet soil,
cypresses raging
your inner vision,
Lear's dream,
nature trembling
before the fate of man,
life-giving fantasies,
wrenched from your brain,
each microcosm,
operating under its own law,
blue, green, a sun of its own,
what must you have seen?

Brought within your prism
we accept the multiplication
of your clear, white light.
We love your "Harvest,"
clear, breathing
its own light,
your still life moves
more than onions,
more than red cabbages should,
in "The Evening,"
light revolving
in a magnetic field,
a galaxy,
infinite movement,
contained
light in your "Potato Eaters,"
making the eye dance,

light glancing
like a billiard ball,
a dot of paint,
light in her eyes,
rebounding, framed
like your soul
in your frame of flesh,
painting green faces
in a green world,
what must you have seen?

Holy Sonnet X

Death, be not proud

John Donne

Death, be not proud, though some have callèd thee
Mighty and dreadful, for thou art not so;
For those who thou think'st thou dost overthrow
Die not, poor Death, nor yet canst thou kill me.
From rest and sleep, which but thy pictures be,
Much pleasure, then from thee much more must flow,
And soonest our best men with thee do go,
Rest of their bones, and souls' delivery.
Thou art slave to fate, chance, kings, and desperate men,
And dost with poison, war, and sickness dwell,
And poppy, or charms can make us sleep as well,
And better than thy stroke; why swell'st thou then?
One short sleep past, we wake eternally,
And Death shall be no more; Death, thou shalt die.

Innocence

(for Tony White)

Thom Gunn

He ran the course and as he ran he grew,
And smelt his fragrance in the field. Already,
Running he knew the most he ever knew,
The egotism of a healthy body.

Ran into manhood, ignorant of the past:
Culture of guilt and guilt's vague heritage,
Self-pity and the soul; what he possessed
Was rich, potential, like the bud's tipped rage.

The Corps developed, it was plain to see,
Courage, endurance, loyalty and skill
To a morale firm as morality,
Hardening him to an instrument, until

The finitude of virtues that were there
Bodied within the swarthy uniform
A compact innocence, child-like and clear,
No doubt could penetrate, no act could harm.

When he stood near the Russian partisan
Being burned alive, he therefore could behold
The ribs wear gently through the darkening skin
And sicken only at the Northern cold,

Could watch the fat burn with a violet flame
And feel disgusted only at the smell,
And judge that all pain finishes the same
As smelting quietly by his boots it fell.

The World Is Too Much with Us

William Wordsworth

The world is too much with us; late and soon,
Getting and spending, we lay waste our powers:
Little we see in Nature that is ours;
We have given our hearts away, a sordid boon!
This Sea that bares her bosom to the moon;
The winds that will be howling at all hours,
And are up-gathered now like sleeping flowers;
For this, for everything, we are out of tune;
It moves us not.—Great God! I'd rather be
A Pagan suckled in a creed outworn;
So might I, standing on this pleasant lea,
Have glimpses that would make me less forlorn;
Have sight of Proteus rising from the sea;
Or hear old Triton blow his wreathèd horn.

152   *The Touch of a Poet*

Full Sky

Jules Supervielle

I had a horse
In a field of the sky
And I plunged
Into the burning daylight.
Nothing stopped me
I moved without knowing,
It was a boat
Rather than a horse,
It was a desire
Rather than a boat,
It was a horse
Such as you never see,
Head of a steed
Blanket of frenzy,
A wind neighing
And spending itself.
I continued to ride
And made signals:
"Follow my tracks,
You can come, My best friends,
The road is open
The sky is clear.
But who is saying this?
I lose sight of myself
In this altitude,
Can you make me out,
I am the man who
Was speaking a minute ago,
Am I still the man
Who is speaking now,
And you, my friends,
Are you the same beings?
One blots out the other
And changes on this ride."

Truth

James Hearst

How the devil do I know
if there are rocks in your field,
plow it and find out.
If the plow strikes something
harder than earth, the point
shatters at a sudden blow
and the tractor jerks sidewise
and dumps you off the seat—
because the spring hitch
isn't set to trip quickly enough
and it never is—probably
you hit a rock. That means
the glacier emptied his pocket
in your field as well as mine,
but the connection with a thing
is the only truth that I know of,
so plow it.

Icarus

Edward Field

Only the feathers floating around the hat
Showed that anything more spectacular had occurred
Than the usual drowning. The police preferred to ignore
The confusing aspects of the case,
And the witnesses ran off to a gang war.
So the report filed and forgotten in the archives read simply
"Drowned," but it was wrong: Icarus
Had swum away, coming at last to the city
Where he rented a house and tended the garden.

"That nice Mr. Hicks" the neighbors called him,
Never dreaming that the gray, respectable suit
Concealed arms that had controlled huge wings
Nor that those sad, defeated eyes had once
Compelled the sun. And had he told them
They would have answered with a shocked, uncomprehending stare.
No, he could not disturb their neat front yards;
Yet all his books insisted that this was a horrible mistake:
What was he doing aging in a suburb?
Can the genius of the hero fall   .
To the middling stature of the merely talented?

And nightly Icarus probes his wound
And daily in his workshop, curtains carefully drawn,
Constructs small wings and tries to fly
To the lighting fixture on the ceiling:
Fails every time and hates himself for trying.

He had thought himself a hero, had acted heroically,
And dreamt of his fall, the tragic fall of the hero;
But now rides commuter trains,
Serves on various committees,
And wishes he had drowned.

The New Icarus

Vassar Miller

Slip off the husk of gravity to lie
Bedded with wind; float on a whimsy, lift
Upon a wish: your bow's own arrow, rift
Newton's decorum—only when you fly.
But naked. No false-feathered fool, you try
Dalliance with heights, nor, plumed with metal, shift
And shear the clouds, imperiling lark and swift
And all birds bridal-bowered in the sky.

Your wreck of bone, barred their delight's dominions,
Lacking their formula for flight, holds imaged
Those alps of air no eagle's wing can quell.
With arms flung crosswise, pinioned to wooden pinions,
You, in one motion plucked and crimson-plumaged,
Outsoar all Heaven, plummeting all Hell.

To A Friend Whose Work Has Come To Triumph

Anne Sexton

Consider Icarus, pasting those sticky wings on,
testing that strange little tug at his shoulder blade,
and think of that first flawless moment over the lawn
of the labyrinth. Think of the difference it made!
There below are the trees, as awkward as camels;
and here are the shocked starlings pumping past
and think of innocent Icarus who is doing quite well:
larger than a sail, over the fog and the blast
of the plushy ocean, he goes. Admire his wings!
Feel the fire at his neck and see how casually
he glances up and is caught, wondrously tunneling
into that hot eye. Who cares that he fell back to the sea?
See him acclaiming the sun and come plunging down
while his sensible daddy goes straight into town.

There Was a Child Went Forth

Walt Whitman

There was a child went forth every day,
And the first object he look'd upon, that object he became,
And that object became part of him for the day or a certain part
 of the day,
Or for many years or stretching cycles of years.

The early lilacs became part of this child,
And grass and white and red morning-glories, and white and red
 clover, and the song of the phoebe-bird,
And the Third-month lambs and the sow's pink-faint litter, and the
 mare's foal and the cow's calf,
And the noisy brood of the barnyard or by the mire of the pond-side,
And the fish suspending themselves so curiously below there, and
 the beautiful curious liquid,
And the water-plants with their graceful flat heads, all became part
 of him.

The field-sprouts of Fourth-month and Fifth-month became part of him,
Winter-grain sprouts and those of the light-yellow corn, and the
 esculent roots of the garden,
And the apple-trees cover'd with blossoms and the fruit afterward,
 and wood-berries, and the commonest weeds by the road,
And the old drunkard staggering home from the out-house of the
 tavern whence he had lately risen,
And the schoolmistress that pass'd on her way to the school,
And the friendly boys that pass'd, and the quarrelsome boys,
And the tidy and fresh-cheek'd girls, and the barefoot negro boy
 and girl,
And all the changes of city and country wherever he went.
His own parents, he that had father'd him and she that had conceiv'd
 him in her womb and birth'd him,
They gave this child more of themselves than that,
They gave him afterward every day, they became part of him.

The mother at home quietly placing the dishes on the supper-table,
The mother with mild words, clean her cap and gown, a wholesome
 odor falling off her person and clothes as she walks by,
The father, strong, self-sufficient, manly, mean, anger'd, unjust,
The blow, the quick loud word, the tight bargain, the crafty lure,
The family usages, the language, the company, the furniture, the
 yearning and swelling heart,

Affection that will not be gainsay'd, the sense of what is real, the
thought if after all it should prove unreal,
The doubts of day-time and the doubts of night-time, the curious
whether and how,
Whether that which appears so is so, or is it all flashes and specks?
Men and women crowding fast in the streets, if they are not flashes
and specks what are they?
The streets themselves and the façades of houses, and goods in
the windows,
Vehicles, teams, the heavy-plank'd wharves, the huge crossing at
the ferries,
The village on the highland seen from afar at sunset, the river between,
Shadows, aureola and mist, the light falling on roofs and gables of
white or brown two miles off,
The schooner near by sleepily dropping down the tide, the little
boat slack-tow'd astern,
The hurrying tumbling waves, quick-broken crests, slapping,
The strata of color'd clouds, the long bar of maroon-tint away
solitary by itself, the spread of purity it lies motionless in,
The horizon's edge, the flying sea-crow, the fragrance of salt marsh
and shore mud,
These became part of that child who went forth every day, and
who now goes, and will always go forth every day.

The Garden of Love

William Blake

I went to the Garden of Love,
And saw what I never had seen:
A chapel was built in the midst,
Where I used to play on the green.

And the gates of this chapel were shut,
And "Thou shalt not" writ over the door;
So I turn'd to the Garden of Love
That so many sweet flowers bore;

And I saw it was filled with graves,
And tomb-stones where flowers should be:
And priests in black gowns were walking their rounds,
And binding with briars my joys and desires.

A Poem to Delight My Friends Who Laugh at Science-Fiction

Edwin Rolfe

That was the year
the small birds in their frail and delicate battalions
committed suicide against the Empire State,
having, in some never-explained manner,
lost their aerial radar, or ignored it.

That was the year
men and women everywhere stopped dying natural deaths.
The agèd, facing sleep, took poison;
the infant, facing life, died with the mother in childbirth;
and the whole wild remainder of the population,
despairing but deliberate, crashed in auto accidents
on roads as clear and uncluttered as ponds.

That was the year every ship on every ocean,
every lake, harbor, river, vanished without trace;
and even ships docked at quays
turned over like harpooned whales, or wounded Normandies.

Yes, and the civilian transcontinental planes
found, like the war-planes, the sky-lanes crowded
and, praising Icarus, plunged to earth in flames.

Many, mild stay-at-homes, slipped in bath tubs,
others, congenital indoors-men, descending stairs,
and some, irrepressible roisterers, playing musical chairs.
Tots fell from scooters cars and tricycles
and casual passersby were stabbed by falling icicles.

Ah, what carnage! It was reported
that even bicarb and aspirin turned fatal,
and seconal too, to those with mild headaches,
whose stomachs were slightly acid, or who found they could not sleep.
All lovers died in bed, as all seafarers on the deep.

Till finally the only people left alive
were the soldiers sullenly spread on battlefields
among the shell-pocked hills and the charred trees.
Thus, even the indispensable wars died of ennui.

But not the expendable conscripts: they remained as always.
However, since no transport was available anywhere,
and home, in any case, was dead, and bare,
the soldiers wandered eternally
in their dazed, early-Chirico landscapes,
like drunken stars in their shrinking orbits
round and round and round and round

and (since I too died in the world-wide suicide)
they may still, for all I know, be there.
Like forsaken chessmen abandoned by paralyzed players,
they may still be there.

A Dirge

Percy Bysshe Shelley

Rough wind, that moanest loud
    Grief too sad for song;
Wild wind, when sullen cloud
    Knells all the night long;
Sad storm, whose tears are vain,
    Bare woods, whose branches strain,
Deep caves and dreary main,—
    Wail, for the world's wrong!

Young and Old

Charles Kingsley

When all the world is young, lad,
    And all the trees are green;
And every goose a swan, lad,
    And every lass a queen;
Then hey for boot and horse, lad,
    And round the world away;
Young blood must have its course, lad,
    And every dog his day.

When all the world is old, lad,
    And all the trees are brown;
And all the sport is stale, lad,
    And all the wheels run down;
Creep home, and take your place there,
    The spent and maimed among:
God grant you find one face there
    You loved when all was young.

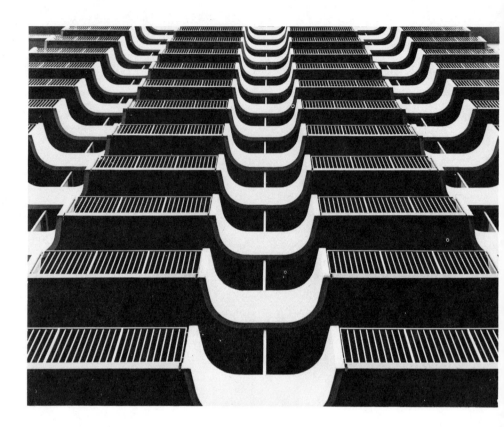

Dolor

Theodore Roethke

I have known the inexorable sadness of pencils,
Neat in their boxes, dolor of pad and paper-weight,
All the misery of manila folders and mucilage,
Desolation in immaculate public places,
Lonely reception room, lavatory, switchboard,
The unalterable pathos of basin and pitcher,
Ritual of multigraph, paper-clip, comma,
Endless duplication of lives and objects.
And I have seen dust from the walls of institutions,
Finer than flour, alive, more dangerous than silica,
Sift, almost invisible, through long afternoons of tedium,
Dropping a fine film on nails and delicate eyebrows,
Glazing the pale hair, the duplicate gray standard faces.

Do Not Go Gentle into That Good Night

Dylan Thomas

Do not go gentle into that good night,
Old age should burn and rave at close of day;
Rage, rage against the dying of the light.

Though wise men at their end know dark is right,
Because their words had forked no lightning they
Do not go gentle into that good night.

Good men, the last wave by, crying how bright
Their frail deeds might have danced in a green bay,
Rage, rage against the dying of the light.

Wild men who caught and sang the sun in flight,
And learn, too late, they grieved it on its way,
Do not go gentle into that good night.

Grave men, near death, who see with blinding sight
Blind eyes could blaze like meteors and be gay,
Rage, rage against the dying of the light.

And you, my father, there on the sad height,
Curse, bless, me now with your fierce tears, I pray.
Do not go gentle into that good night.
Rage, rage against the dying of the light.

Tombstone with Cherubim

Horace Gregory

No notice in the papers:
                              a cold voice over the telephone
saying she was dead.
                    Somebody whispered, "Syphilis,"
a sentimental lie.
                    Somebody said,
"She was rococo, a Florentine olive tree
cut down and stripped beneath the body
of a football-captain-stock-broker asleep
upon Miami sands."
                         "She shrieked at poverty.
Divorced from silk, furs, and patented nickel-plated
limousines."
                    She loved unsought, relaxed security
drifting to bed with men as though they were
exotic dreams.
                    "Damn Marie,
you should have gone out like a row of mazda lamps
smashed with a crowbar."
                              These were the legends.

The facts are these:
(true enough for a beautiful girl
who held a glimpse of midnight in her hair)
I saw her pacing with unforgettable ease
down Michigan Boulevard one autumn morning.

                    She died in Lesbian serenity
neither hot nor cold
                    until the chaste limbs stiffened.
Disconnect the telephone. Cut the wires.

r-p-o-p-h-e-s-s-a-g-r

e. e. cummings

```
                    r-p-o-p-h-e-s-s-a-g-r
                who
a)s w(e loo)k
upnowgath
        PPEGORHRASS
                        eringint(o-.
    aThe):l
        eA
            !p:
S                                        a
                (r
rIvInG              .gRrEaPsPhOs)
                                    to
rea(be)rran(com)gi(e)ngly
,grasshopper;
```

The Applicant

Sylvia Plath

First, are you our sort of a person?
Do you wear
A glass eye, false teeth or a crutch,
A brace or a hook,
Rubber breasts or a rubber crotch,

Stitches to show something's missing? No, no? Then
How can we give you a thing?
Stop crying.
Open your hand.
Empty? Empty. Here is a hand

To fill it and willing
To bring teacups and roll away headaches
And do whatever you tell it.
Will you marry it?
It is guaranteed

To thumb shut your eyes at the end
And dissolve of sorrow.
We make new stock from the salt.
I notice you are stark naked.
How about this suit—

Black and stiff, but not a bad fit.
Will you marry it?
It is waterproof, shatterproof, proof
Against fire and bombs through the roof.
Believe me, they'll bury you in it.

Now your head, excuse me, is empty.
I have the ticket for that.
Come here, sweetie, out of the closet.
Well, what do you think of *that?*
Naked as paper to start

But in twenty-five years she'll be silver,
In fifty, gold.
A living doll, everywhere you look.
It can sew, it can cook,
It can talk, talk, talk.

It works, there is nothing wrong with it.
You have a hole, it's a poultice.
You have an eye, it's an image.
My boy, it's your last resort.
Will you marry it, marry it, marry it.

Her Story

Naomi Long Madgett

They gave me the wrong name, in the first place.
They named me Grace and waited for a light and agile dancer.
But some trick of the genes mixed me up
And instead I turned out big and black and burly.

In the second place, I fashioned the wrong dreams.
I wanted to dress like Juliet and act
Before applauding audiences on Broadway.
I learned more about Shakespeare than he knew about himself.
But of course, all that was impossible.
"Talent, yes," they would tell me,
"But an actress has to look the part."
So I ended up waiting on tables in Harlem
And hearing uncouth men yell at me:
"Hey, momma, you can cancel that hamburger
And come on up to 102."

In the third place, I tried the wrong solution.
The stuff I drank made me deathly sick
And someone called a doctor
Next time I'll try a gun.

Dover Beach

Matthew Arnold

The sea is calm to-night,
The tide is full, the moon lies fair
Upon the straits;—on the French coast, the light
Gleams and is gone; the cliffs of England stand,
Glimmering and vast, out in the tranquil bay.
Come to the window, sweet is the night-air!
Only, from the long life of spray
Where the sea meets the moon-blanched land,
Listen! you hear the grating roar
Of pebbles which the waves draw back, and fling,
At their return, up the high strand,
Begin, and cease, and then again begin,
With tremulous cadence slow, and bring
The eternal note of sadness in.

Sophocles long ago
Heard it on the Aegean, and it brought
Into his mind the turbid ebb and flow
Of human misery; we
Find also in the sound a thought,
Hearing it by this distant northern sea.

The Sea of Faith
Was once, too, at the full, and round earth's shore
Lay like the folds of a bright girdle furled.
But now I only hear
Its melancholy, long, withdrawing roar,
Retreating, to the breath
Of the night-wind, down the vast edges drear
And naked shingles of the world.

Ah, love, let us be true
To one another! for the world, which seems
To lie before us like a land of dreams,
So various, so beautiful, so new,
Hath really neither joy, nor love, nor light,
Nor certitude, nor peace, nor help for pain;
And we are here as on a darkling plain
Swept with confused alarms of struggle and flight,
Where ignorant armies clash by night.

Ode

Intimations Of Immortality From Recollections Of Early Childhood

William Wordsworth

> The Child is father of the Man;
> And I could wish my days to be
> Bound each to each by natural piety.

I

There was a time when meadow, grove, and stream,
The earth, and every common sight,
        To me did seem
        Appareled in celestial light,
The glory and the freshness of a dream.
It is not now as it hath been of yore—
        Turn whereso'er I may,
            By night or day,
The things which I have seen I now can see no more.

II

        The Rainbow comes and goes,
        And lovely is the Rose,
        The Moon doth with delight
Look round her when the heavens are bare,
        Waters on a starry night
        Are beautiful and fair;
    The sunshine is a glorious birth;
    But yet I know, where'er I go,
That there hath passed away a glory from the earth.

III

Now, while the birds thus sing a joyous song,
    And while the young lambs bound
        As to the tabor's sound,
To me alone there came a thought of grief:
A timely utterance gave that thought relief,
        And I again am strong:
The cataracts blow their trumpets from the steep;
No more shall grief of mine the season wrong;

I hear the Echoes through the mountains throng,
The Winds come to me from the fields of sleep,
    And all the earth is gay;
        Land and sea
  Give themselves up to jollity,
    And with the heart of May
Doth every Beast keep holiday—
    Thou Child of Joy,
Shout round me, let me hear thy shouts, thou happy Shepherd-boy!

IV

Ye blessèd Creatures, I have heard the call
  Ye to each other make; I see
The heavens laugh with you in your jubilee;
    My heart is at your festival,
    My head hath its coronal,
The fullness of your bliss, I feel—I feel it all.
      Oh, evil day! if I were sullen
      While Earth herself is adorning,
        This sweet May morning,
      And the Children are culling
        On every side,
    In a thousand valleys far and wide,
    Fresh flowers; while the sun shines warm,
And the Babe leaps up on his Mother's arm—
    I hear, I hear, with joy I hear!
    —But there's a Tree, of many, one,
A single Field which I have looked upon,
Both of them speak of something that is gone:
      The Pansy at my feet
      Doth the same tale repeat:
Whither is fled the visionary gleam?
Where is it now, the glory and the dream?

V

Our birth is but a sleep and a forgetting:
The Soul that rises with us, our life's Star,
    Hath had elsewhere its setting,
    And cometh from afar:
    Not in entire forgetfulness,
    And not in utter nakedness,
But trailing clouds of glory do we come
    From God, who is our home:
Heaven lies about us in our infancy!
Shades of the prison-house begin to close
    Upon the growing Boy

But he
Beholds the light, and whence it flows,
    He sees it in his joy;
The Youth, who daily farther from the east
    Must travel, still is Nature's Priest,
    And by the vision splendid
    Is on his way attended;
At length the Man perceives it die away,
And fade into the light of common day.

VI

Earth fills her lap with pleasures of her own;
Yearnings she hath in her own natural kind,
And, even with something of a Mother's mind,
    And no unworthy aim,
    The homely Nurse doth all she can
To make her foster child, her Inmate Man,
    Forget the glories he hath known,
And that imperial palace whence he came.

VII

Behold the Child among his newborn blisses,
A six-years' Darling of a pygmy size!
See, where 'mid work of his own hand he lies,
Fretted by sallies of his mother's kisses,
With light upon him from his father's eyes!
See, at his feet, some little plan or chart,
Some fragment from his dream of human life,
Shaped by himself with newly-learnèd art;
    A wedding or a festival,
    A mourning or a funeral;
        And this hath now his heart,
    And unto this he frames his song;
        Then will be fit his tongue
To dialogues of business, love, or strife;
        But it will not be long
        Ere this be thrown aside,
        And with new joy and pride
The little Actor cons another part;
Filling from time to time his "humorous stage"
With all the Persons, down to palsied Age,
That Life brings with her in her equipage;
        As if his whole vocation
        Were endless imitation.

VIII

Thou, whose exterior semblance doth belie
 Thy Soul's immensity;
Thou best Philosopher, who yet dost keep
Thy heritage, thou Eye among the blind,
That, deaf and silent, read'st the eternal deep,
Haunted forever by the eternal mind—
 Mighty Prophet! Seer blest!
 On whom those truths do rest,
Which we are toiling all our lives to find,
In darkness lost, the darkness of the grave;
Thou, over whom thy Immortality
Broods like the Day, a Master o'er a Slave,
A Presence which is not to be put by;
Thou little Child, yet glorious in the might
Of heaven-born freedom on thy being's height,
Why with such earnest pains dost thou provoke
The years to bring the inevitable yoke,
Thus blindly with thy blessedness at strife?
Full soon thy Soul shall have her earthly freight,
And custom lie upon thee with a weight,
Heavy as frost, and deep almost as life!

IX

 O joy! that in our embers
 Is something that doth live,
 That nature yet remembers
 What was so fugitive!
The thought of our past years in me doth breed
Perpetual benediction: not indeed
For that which is most worthy to be blest;
Delight and liberty, the simple creed
Of Childhood, whether busy or at rest,
With new-fledged hope still fluttering in his breast—
 Not for these I raise
 The song of thanks and praise;
 But for those obstinate questionings
 Of sense and outward things,
 Fallings from us, vanishings;
 Blank misgivings of a Creature
Moving about in worlds not realized,
High instincts before which our mortal Nature
Did tremble like a guilty Thing surprised;
 But for those first affections,
 Those shadowy recollections,

Which, be they what they may,
Are yet the fountain light of all our day,
Are yet a master light of all our seeing;
      Uphold us, cherish, and have power to make
Our noisy years seem moments in the being
Of the eternal Silence: truths that wake,
            To perish never;
Which neither listlessness, nor mad endeavor,
            Nor Man nor Boy,
Nor all that is at enmity with joy,
Can utterly abolish or destroy!
            Hence in a season of calm weather
            Though inland far we be,
Our Souls have sight of that immortal sea
            Which brought us hither,
            Can in a moment travel thither,
And see the Children sport upon the shore,
And hear the mighty waters rolling evermore.

X

Then sing, ye Birds, sing, sing a joyous song!
            And let the young Lambs bound
            As to the tabor's sound!
We in thought will join your throng,
            Ye that pipe and ye that play,
            Ye that through your hearts today
            Feel the gladness of the May!
What though the radiance which was once so bright
Be now forever taken from my sight,
      Though nothing can bring back the hour
Of splendor in the grass, of glory in the flower;
            We will grieve not, rather find
            Strength in what remains behind;
            In the primal sympathy
            Which having been must ever be;
            In the soothing thoughts that spring
            Out of human suffering;
            In the faith that looks through death,
In years that bring the philosophic mind.

XI

And O, ye Fountains, Meadows, Hills, and Groves,
Forebode not any severing of our loves!
Yet in my heart of hearts I feel your might;
I only have relinguished one delight
To live beneath your more habitual sway.

I love the Brooks which down their channels fret,
Even more than when I tripped lightly as they;
The innocent brightness of a newborn Day
      Is lovely yet;
The clouds that gather round the setting sun
Do take a sober coloring from an eye
That hath kept watch o'er man's mortality;
Another race hath been, and other palms are won.
Thanks to the human heart by which we live,
Thanks to its tenderness, its joys, and fears,
To me the meanest flower that blows can give
Thoughts that do often lie too deep for tears.

Sensorium

The following poems have purposely not been put into any of the four categories. We want *you* to read them and, based on your own reactions, put each poem into the category *you* think most appropriate. But first and foremost, *enjoy them.*

The Naked and the Nude

Robert Graves

For me, the naked and the nude
(By lexicographers construed
As synonyms that should express
The same deficiency of dress
Or shelter) stand as wide apart
As love from lies, or truth from art.

Lovers without reproach will gaze
On bodies naked and ablaze;
The hippocratic eye will see
In nakedness, anatomy;
And naked shines the Goddess when
She mounts her lion among men.

The nude are bold, the nude are sly
To hold each treasonable eye.
While draping by a showman's trick
Their dishabille in rhetoric,
They grin a mock-religious grin
Of scorn at those of naked skin.

The naked, therefore, who compete
Against the nude may know defeat;
Yet when they both together tread
The briary pastures of the dead,
By Gorgons with long whips pursued,
How naked go the sometime nude!

Sonnet 30

William Shakespeare

When to the sessions of sweet silent thought
I summon up remembrance of things past,
I sigh the lack of many a thing I sought
And with old woes new wail my dear time's waste;
Then can I drown an eye unused to flow,
For precious friends hid in death's dateless night,
And weep afresh love's long since cancelled woe,
And moan the expense of many a vanished sight;
Then can I grieve at grievances foregone,
And heavily from woe to woe tell o'er
The sad account of fore-bemoanèd moan,
Which I new pay as if not paid before:
    But if the while I think on thee, dear friend,
    All losses are restored, and sorrows end.

Life Cycle of Common Man

Howard Nemerov

Roughly figured, this man of moderate habits,
This average consumer of the middle class,
Consumed in the course of his average life span
Just under half a million cigarettes,
Four thousand fifths of gin and about
A quarter as much vermouth; he drank
Maybe a hundred thousand cups of coffee,
And counting his parents' share it cost
Something like half a million dollars
To put him through life. How many beasts
Died to provide him with meat, belts and shoes
Cannot be certainly said.

         But anyhow,
It is in this way that a man travels through time,
Leaving behind him a lengthening trail
Of empty bottles and bones, of broken shoes,
Frayed collars and worn out or outgrown
Diapers and dinnerjackets, silk ties and slickers.

Given the energy and security thus achieved,
He did . . . ? What? The usual things, of course,
The eating, dreaming, drinking and begetting,
And he worked for the money which was to pay
For the eating, et cetera, which were necessary
If he were to go on working for the money, et cetera,
But chiefly he talked. As the bottles and bones
Accumulated behind him, the words proceeded
Steadily from the front of his face as he
Advanced into silence and made it verbal.
Who can tally the tale of his words? A lifetime
Would barely suffice for their repetition;
If you merely printed all his commas the result
Would be a very large volume, and the number of times
He said "thank you" or "very little sugar, please,"
Would stagger the imagination. There were also
Witticisms, platitudes, and statements beginning
"It seems to me" or "As I always say."

Consider the courage in all that, and behold the man
Walking into deep silence, with the ectoplastic

Cartoon's balloon of speech proceeding
Steadily out of the front of his face, the words
Borne along on the breath which is his spirit
Telling the numberless tale of his untold Word
Which makes the world his apple, and forces him to eat.

My parents kept me from children who were rough

Stephen Spender

My parents kept me from children who were rough
Who threw words like stones and who wore torn clothes.
Their thighs showed through rags. They ran in the street
And climbed cliffs and stripped by the country streams.

I feared more than tigers their muscles like iron
Their jerking hands and their knees tight on my arms.
I feared the salt coarse pointing of those boys
Who copied my lisp behind me on the road.

They were lithe, they sprang out behind hedges
Like dogs to bark at my world. They threw mud
While I looked the other way, pretending to smile.
I longed to forgive them, but they never smiled.

A Supermarket in California

Allen Ginsberg

What thoughts I have of you tonight, Walt Whitman, for I walked down the side-streets under the trees with a headache self-conscious looking at the full moon.

In my hungry fatigue, and shopping for images, I went into the neon fruit supermarket, dreaming of your enumerations!

What peaches and what penumbras! Whole families shopping at night! Aisles full of husbands! Wives in the avocados, babies in the tomatoes!—and you, Garcia Lorca, what were you doing down by the watermelons?

I saw you, Walt Whitman, childless, lonely old grubber, poking among the meats in the refrigerator and eyeing the grocery boys.

I heard you asking questions of each: Who killed the pork chops? What price bananas? Are you my Angel?

I wandered in and out of the brilliant stacks of cans following you, and followed in my imagination by the store detective.

We strode down the open corridors together in our solitary fancy tasting artichokes, possessing every frozen delicacy, and never passing the cashier.

Where are we going, Walt Whitman? The doors close in an hour. Which way does your beard point tonight?

(I touch your book and dream of our odyssey in the supermarket and feel absurd.)

Will we walk all night through solitary streets? The trees add shade to shade, lights out in the houses, we'll both be lonely.

Will we stroll dreaming of the lost America of love past blue automobiles in driveways, home to our silent cottage?

Ah, dear father, graybeard, lonely old courage-teacher, what America did you have when Charon quit poling his ferry and you got out on a smoking bank and stood watching the boat disappear on the black waters of Lethe?

Who Hurt You So?

Edna St. Vincent Millay

Who hurt you so,
My dear?
Who, long ago
When you were very young,
Did, said, became, was . . . something that you did not know
Beauty could ever do, say, be, become?—
So that your brown eyes filled
With tears they never, not to this day, have shed . . .
Not because one more boy stood hurt by life,
No: because something deathless had dropped dead—
An ugly, an indecent thing to do—
So that you stood and stared, with open mouth in which the tongue
Froze slowly backward toward its root,
As if it would not speak again, too badly stung
By memories thick as wasps about a nest invaded
To know if or if not you suffered pain.

Mementos, 1

W. D. Snodgrass

Sorting out letters and piles of my old
   Canceled checks, old clippings, and yellow note cards
That meant something once, I happened to find
   Your picture. *That* picture. I stopped there cold,
Like a man raking piles of dead leaves in his yard
      Who has turned up a severed hand.

Still, that first second, I was glad: you stand
   Just as you stood—shy, delicate, slender,
In that long gown of green lace netting and daisies
   That you wore to our first dance. The sight of you stunned
Us all. Well, our needs were different, then,
      And our ideals came easy.

Then through the war and those two long years
   Overseas, the Japanese dead in their shacks
Among dishes, dolls, and lost shoes; I carried
   This glimpse of you, there, to choke down my fear,
Prove it has been, that it might come back.
      That was before we got married.

—Before we drained out one another's force
   With lies, self-denial, unspoken regret
And the sick eyes that blame; Before the divorce
   And the treachery. Say it: before we met. Still,
I put back your picture. Someday, in due course,
      I will find that it's still there.

On His Blindness

John Milton

When I consider how my light is spent
  Ere half my days in this dark world and wide,
  And that one talent which is death to hide
  Lodged with me useless, though my soul more bent
To serve therewith my Maker, and present
  My true account, lest He returning chide,
  "Doth God exact day-labor, light denied?"
  I fondly ask. But Patience, to prevent
That murmur, soon replies, "God doth not need
  Either man's work or his own gifts. Who best
  Bear his mild yoke, they serve him best. His state
Is kingly: thousands at his bidding speed,
  And post o'er land and ocean without rest;
  They also serve who only stand and wait."

The Portrait

Stanley Kunitz

My mother never forgave my father
for killing himself,
especially at such an awkward time
and in a public park,
that spring
when I was waiting to be born.
She locked his name in her deepest cabinet
and would not let him out,
though I could hear him thumping.
When I came down from the attic
with the pastel portrait in my hand
of a long-lipped stranger
with a brave moustache
and deep brown level eyes,
she ripped it into shreds
without a single word
and slapped me hard.
In my sixty-fourth year
I can feel my cheek
still burning.

Sonnets from the Portuguese
XIV

Elizabeth Barrett Browning

If thou must love me, let it be for naught
Except for love's sake only. Do not say,
"I love her for her smile—her look—her way
Of speaking gently,—for a trick of thought
That falls in well with mine, and certes brought
A sense of pleasant ease on such a day"—
For these things in themselves, Belovèd, may
Be changed, or change for thee—and love, so wrought,
May be unwrought so. Neither love me for
Thine own dear pity's wiping my cheeks dry:
A creature might forget to weep, who bore
Thy comfort long, and lose thy love thereby!
But love me for love's sake, that evermore
Thou mayst love on, through love's eternity.

The Teacher

Erica Jong

The teacher stands before the class.
She's talking of Chaucer.
But the students aren't hungry for Chaucer.
They want to devour her.
They are eating her knees, her toes, her breasts, her eyes
& spitting out
her words.
What do they want with words?
They want a real lesson!

She is naked before them.
Psalms are written on her thighs.
When she walks, sonnets divide
into octaves & sestets.
Couplets fall into place
when her fingers nervously toy
with the chalk.

But the words don't clothe her.
No amount of poetry can save her now.
There's no volume big enough to hide in.
No unabridged Webster, no OED.

The students aren't dumb.
They want a lesson.
Once they might have taken life
by the scruff of its neck
in a neat couplet.
But now
they need blood.
They have left Chaucer alone
& have eaten the teacher.

She's gone now.
Nothing remains
but a page of print.
She's past our helping.
Perhaps she's part of her students.
(Don't ask how.)

Eat this poem.

today is a day of great joy

Victor Hernandez Cruz

when they stop poems
in the mail   & clap
their hands & dance to
them
when women become pregnant
by the side of poems
the strongest sounds   making
the river go along

it is a great day

as poems fall down to
movie crowds   in restaurants
in bars

when poems start to
knock down walls   to
choke politicians
when poems scream &
begin to break the air

that is the time of
true poets   that is
the time of greatness

a true poet   aiming
poems   & watching things
fall to the ground

it is a great day.

Postscript

Our revels now are ended. These our actors,
As I foretold you, were all spirits, and
Are melted into air, into thin air;
And, like the baseless fabric of this vision,
The cloud-capp'd towers, the gorgeous palaces,
The solemn temples, the great globe itself,
Yea, all which it inherit, shall dissolve;
And, like this insubstantial pageant faded,
Leave not a rack behind. We are such stuff
As dreams are made on, and our little life
Is rounded with a sleep.

William Shakespeare, The Tempest, act 4, scene 1.

Handbook

Joey Tranchina, Student Editor
San Francisco State University

Paul C. Holmes
College of San Mateo

I for one cannot lose the belief that
it is more important to experience the poem
than to judge it . . . to read a poem,
come prepared for delight.   *John Ciardi*

Preface to Handbook

Apart from all the reasons why people *might* read poetry, I believe there is one main reason people *do* read poetry: They need to feel real communication with another human being. We all must have a way to share our private thoughts and feelings if we are to live fulfilled lives. Writing poetry is one way to share communication; reading it, really listening to it, is another.

I listened to the poems in this anthology, then wrote responses and often questions about points I considered important. Every idea about a poem is small in comparison to the beauty of its song; every approach is limited. Within my limits, I hope that the questions in this handbook will help you hear the poems more deeply and clearly. In answering the questions, you will see some of the things that are going on in each poem; but do not stop with my questions. They are tiny signs pointing toward a road that can lead you to greater insights . . . so, ENJOY!

Joey Tranchina

Photographs

Both photographs and poems have the power to evoke feelings. Several of the poems in this anthology were accompanied by photographs. Look back at any one of them. Does the tone of the photograph relate to the tone of the poem?[1] How? What did you feel when you looked at the photograph? Can you relate that feeling to the feeling you got when you read the poem? Discuss the similarities and differences between the two art forms.

---

[1] By *tone* we mean the poet's or photographer's attitude toward his theme and toward the reader or viewer.

Constantly Risking Absurdity

Lawrence Ferlinghetti

(Page 3)

I read this poem three times aloud before it came together for me. It's important to read a poem until it makes sense before you try to form an opinion or answer any questions about it—or even ask any questions about it.

1. What are "sleight-of-foot tricks"? What does "entrechats" mean? What is "absurdity"? Who is "a little charleychaplin man"? What I'm really asking by these short questions is: Have you read the poem? No matter how many deeper things the poem can say to you, it seems best to start by asking: What does the poet mean by the words he uses?

2. When a poet paints a picture with words, it is called an *image*. What image does Lawrence Ferlinghetti use to portray his view of the poet?

3. Knowing the formal names for various forms of expression is not nearly as important as enjoying the poem, but it does have a certain value when we want to discuss the way a poem works. With this in mind, what kind of image is used in line 6? In other words, what is it called when the poet says _____ is like _____?

4. How important does Lawrence Ferlinghetti consider the poet's performance?

5. What does he consider to be the job of the poet?

Poems

Peter Kelso

(Page 4)

1. Did this poem change for you when you read the age of the poet? How?
2. How does this poem appeal to your eye? In which lines does he try to reach you through your ear?

3. How does Peter Kelso define poetry?

4. Phrases like "haunt the heart" and "magical, mysterious / Mirages"[2] are part of the music of poety called *alliteration*. (Alliteration is the repetition of an initial sound in two or more words of a phase.) How does the music of alliteration add to the meaning of the poem?

5. Why do you think this poem was placed at the beginning of the book?

---

[2]The solidus (/) is used to indicate the end of a line of verse when quoting.

Poetry

Marianne Moore

(Page 5)

1. According to Marianne Moore, poetry can be "useful." What's useful about it?

2. What is a half poet?

3. The poet knows we "do not admire what / we cannot understand." What does Marianne Moore do to make us understand this poem? Or, to put it another way: Some poetry is music for the ear; some poetry brings visions to our eyes; other poetry puts thoughts in our minds. From which of these does she try to reach us to make us feel the poem?

4. This poem expresses a sense of values. What do you feel about the poet's use of the word "genuine"?

5. Why does Marianne Moore dislike poetry; or, what does she dislike about it?

Poetry Liberation

Jean Pumphrey

(Page 6)

1. Consider the images in this poem. Is the poet concerned primarily with ideas and essence? With images and particulars? With all of these? Consider how the poet's point of view differs from the point of view of the "Sir" in the poem.

2. To define is to exclude, and attempts to define poetry are inevitably limiting. Poetry eludes definition just as the living breath defies exact description. How does the "Sir" in the poem attempt to define poetry? How successful is his definition? Can you think of a good, workable definition of poetry?

3. Poetry is twice referred to in the poem as "she". Do you think of poetry as being feminine? Whatever you conclude, it is certain that definitions of femininity vary considerably as do definitions of poetry. How does the "lady" described in the last two lines of the poem differ from "Sir's" definition of poetry? What is feminine?

4. The line "without a ripple" appears twice in the poem. What, if anything, does this repetition add to the poem? Contrast "without a ripple" with "gallops away."

In My Craft or Sullen Art

Dylan Thomas

(Page 7)

1. What does "spindrift" mean?

2. What is a craft? What is an art? Is poetry a craft or an art? What increased perspective is added here by comparing the two? Why?

3. What reason does Dylan Thomas give for writing poetry? What does he say with his image of the lovers? Does he mean only "lovers" or is he reaching deeper?

4. The poet lists many things that do not motivate him to write. What are they? Who is the "proud man apart / From the raging moon"? Who are the "towering dead"?

5. Is it okay that lovers "pay no praise or wages / Nor heed my craft or art"? Could the writing of poetry, like the singing of songs, be so enjoyable and satisfying in itself that it demands no reward? Li Po (d. 762 A.D.), one of the greatest poets of all time in any language, while sitting on the banks of a river would write poem after poem, he would make little boats out of the paper, which he would sail downstream. Do you think this is how Dylan Thomas felt about his craft-art?

Gentle

Touch Tenderly

Helen Berryhill

(Page 11)

1. Touch what tenderly? Touch life? Touch the poet? Touch each other! Depending on which of the decisions you make about this, you touch three different poems. But is poetry about decisions? Is it possible that the poet was commenting on all three, that because of the richness of poetry she did not have to pick one or another but could really speak of all three *levels* of meaning at once?

2. "This frightened fawn / Meadowed in your grasp": How do you respond to the words used to make this image?

3. What do the recurring lines "When you touch— / If you touch" add to the poem?

4. Underline the words in the poem that convey to you that you are handling something fragile.

5. Pick out the words that describe different ways of touching.

Sonnet 18

William Shakespeare

(Page 13)

The best advice I can offer about Shakespeare's *Sonnet 18* is to commit it to memory. It takes a while to find out how good he really is. Because of the time gap between today and Elizabethan England (1558–1603), when Shakespeare wrote, it takes a little effort to understand and appreciate his poetry. To overcome this for myself, I got a recording of the sonnets and one of a good production of *Hamlet* from the library and played them over and over with the text in front of me until I began to understand and get a feeling for them.

1. Huey Newton, the Black Panther leader, said that he taught himself to read literature in the penitentiary by reading *Hamlet* and *Macbeth* over and over. Why is it significant that a black leader would use Shakespeare to learn how to read literature? Why is Shakespeare worth such effort? Perhaps it is because once you delve into his dramas and/or poetry you recognize a universal truth about the human condition that many people (regardless of race, religion, or nationality) have experienced deeply. Although the poet uses sixteenth-century language to express his ideas, once you get past that and into the truth he is talking about, it is well worth the effort.

Here are some more guidelines: A sonnet is a 14-line poem; Shakespeare usually stated a question somewhere in the first 12 lines and then answered it in the last two.[3] A Sonnet has a specific *rhyme scheme* (a pattern of rhyming in a series of lines, a stanza, or a whole poem). This particular sonnet has the following rhyme scheme: a b a b, c d c d, e f e f, g g; it is called an English, or Shakespearean, sonnet. Copy this rhyme scheme on the lines of Shakespeare's *Sonnet 18*. Why are lines 1 and 3 marked a, lines 2 and 4 marked b, and so on?

2. Why do you suppose many poets continue to write in set forms? (Set forms probably began as a way of making it easier for the reader to memorize the lines.)

3. Why do you suppose love is such a common theme in poetry?

This Is Just To Say

William Carlos Williams

(Page 14)

1. A lot of so-called biographical data is often irrelevant to a richer reading of a poem. But would it help you to know that William Carlos Williams actually left this poem in a friend's icebox after eating plums? Discuss the naturalness of this poem. Its words are not "poetic," but are plain, ordinary, everyday words.

2. Describe the language used in this poem.

3. What makes this language poetry?

4. William Carlos Williams (1883–1963) was a physician who delivered babies in Patterson, New Jersey. Locate and read more of his poetry. Can you relate your ideas of life as a doctor to his sort of poetry? This is asking for what you can infer from the words of the poems themselves, not from any research into his life. What does the way he writes tell us about the man?

---

[3]Two successive line of verse, usually in the same meter, whose end words rhyme (as do the last two in this sonnet) are called a *couplet.*

A Jellyfish

Marianne Moore

(Page 15)

1. What does the poet imply when she says "fluctuating charm"?

2. In "an amber-tinctured amethyst / inhabits it" she repeats the sounds "a" and "t". This is one of the ways a poet brings out the music in words. It is called *alliteration*. What effect does this alliteration have?

3. Marianne Moore is telling a story about an encounter with a jellyfish. What do you know about jellyfish that would cause this response? If this is about more than jellyfish, what might she be saying?

To Be in Love

Gwendolyn Brooks

(Page 17)

1. This poem pictures a love relationship. Can you follow the progress of this experience as described in the poem?

2. Do any of the lines strike you as being particularly beautiful, far more lovely than the rest of the poem? If so, what are they?

3. According to this poet, how does being "in love" affect the personality? Does she make any judgment as to whether these effects are good or bad?

4. What is meant by "To apprize / Is to mesmerize"?

5. A person writing poems or songs must say clearly in a few words what he or she has to say. Would you say that Gwendolyn Brooks achieved an effective economy of words in this poem?

in Just—   spring

e. e. cummings

(Page 18)

1. e. e. cummings loved to play with words. This works especially exciting word magic in a poem about children and spring. Briefly describe what is happening with the children in this poem.

2. The poet is famous for using unconventional punctuation and running words together. Locate some of these run-together words. What is their function in the poem?

3. When you read this poem aloud, what does the rhythm sound like? Does it fit a poem about children playing in spring? What sounds in the poem convey the sounds of children playing?

4. Locate the three references to the "balloonman" in this poem. How does the poet change the "balloonman's" image in each of them?

Sonnet 29

William Shakespeare

(Page 19)

Shakespeare again!

Since I believe that hearing what Shakespeare wrote is more important than anything we could say about it, I would ask you to learn this poem by heart and recite it rather than answer any questions about it. If you feel that memorizing anything is torture, I'd ask you to read this poem aloud until you believe you could give it a good reading. Hopefully, this will help you enjoy the poem and understand what Shakespeare was trying to say.

I Saw in Louisiana a Live-Oak Growing

Walt Whitman

(Page 21)

1. How does it affect your reading of a poem when you do not need a dictionary to look up even one word? What does that tell you about the poem? Who does the poet see as his audience?

2. What is the central theme of this poem, that is, what is Walt Whitman saying?

3. The poet says he broke off a twig, a "curious token," which makes him think of "manly love." Can you see this entire poem as a "token," something the poet wrote to remind others or himself of the power of this experience?

4. In what terms does the poet describe himself?

5. Describe how Whitman compares, then contrasts, himself with this oak tree growing in Louisiana.

When I Am Not With You

Sara Teasdale

(Page 22)

1. In many parts of the world (especially India), there is a tradition whereby a young woman writes a song—both to her lover and to her God—expressing physical and religious love. Buffy St. Marie uses this technique often in her songs. Can you see that the words in Sara Teasdale's poem could be spoken as a love song or a prayer?

2. Describe the style in which the poem is written. Is it effective in making her feelings and experiences memorable to you?

3. "poor pride bows down / Like grass in a rain storm": What does this mean?

Where Have You Gone?

Mari E. Evans

(Page 23)

1. This poem is very much like *When I Am Not With You*—and yet so different. Discuss the similarities and differences.

2. One of the good things about poetry is its surprises. What did you find surprising in this poem? How did the poet build the poem to emphasize the surprise?

The River-Merchant's Wife: A Letter

Ezra Pound

(Page 25)

1. This poem is a personal favorite of mine. There are so many good things in it that I will have difficulty deciding which to call to your attention. This poem is like the work of a master tapestry weaver who has taken many intricate patterns and woven them skillfully into one bold design. Read it aloud three or four times. Notice how many of the images relate to nature.

2. This poem was translated by Pound from the Chinese of Rihaku, one of the greatest poets of the T'ang Dynasty, Li Po (700–762). My friends who speak Chinese, however, say that this is not so much a translation as a recreation, a poem given inspiration by the Chinese. Part of the inspiration is in the use of Chinese images. For example, what do you think it means to have hair "still cut straight across my forehead"?

3. What does "I looked at the wall. / Called to, a thousand times, I never looked back" mean?

Are you puzzled about the line "Why should I climb the look out?" It was once explained to me that a lookout was a high place where women whose husbands were late returning from the sea would pray and wait for them.

4. When you are supposed to pause at the end of a line of poetry, it is usually indicated by a comma or a period, this is called an *end-stopped* line. When you are supposed to continue reading into the next line without pause, it is called a *run-on* line. Locate in this poem examples of an end-stopped line and a run-on line. What is the effect of these two kinds of endings? Does it make a difference? How would it affect this poem if run-on lines predominated? Would you know where the lines ended? Would it make any difference? How would it affect your understanding?

5. Although the poem is written in English, the poet is able to give the reader the impression that he is reading it in the original Chinese. What devices does the poet use to convey this impression?

My Heart Leaps Up

William Wordsworth

(Page 26)

1. "The Child is father of the Man" is one of the most famous lines in all of English literature. Why do you think it has stood out in so many people's memories? In general, what is there about a few lines or a phrase in poetry or prose that makes it stick in the memory so that we look at it and look at it until we look at life through it?

2. Now that we have established that this line is so famous, and you have thought about why that's so, what does the poet mean when he says "The Child is father of the Man"?

3. There is a lot in this poem about joy in nature. What did Wordsworth mean by "natural piety"? Can you relate this feeling about nature to your own idea of the word piety?

4. The poet considers this feeling with nature so important that he would choose to die rather than live without it. What does he tell us about this feeling in these few words? How can you know what he feels from the evidence of these few words?

5. This poem seems to be an expression of a totally spontaneous joy in nature, yet it is written in a rhyme scheme (*a b, c c, a b c d d*). Why do you think a poem expressing this sort of feeling would be so formal or have any form at all? Could it be that poets use form because it helps communicate their message?

In a Station of the Metro

Ezra Pound

(Page 27)

This is probably the best example, in English, for showing that the number of words used in a poem bears no relationship to the importance of that poem. Poems—like diamonds—can be weighed, but their true value becomes apparent only when we appraise their depth, color, and clarity. This poem came out of the "imagist" movement: a time when a group of important poets worked to achieve visual images with their words. Do you get the picture?

1. The Metro is the subway in Paris. Does that make the picture any clearer?

2. If Ezra Pound were concerned only with the visual, he could have written "petals on a damp, dark branch." What would have been lost?

3. What do you feel Ezra Pound is saying about human beings in this word picture?

4. Do you think you'll remember this poem? Why?

Afterwards

Thomas Hardy

(Page 28)

1. This is a strong poem that takes awhile to get into. What is a "postern"? What does the poet mean by "tremulous stay"? What is the "dewfall-hawk"? What does "furtively" mean? What are the "full-starred heavens that winter sees"? As each one of these images adds to your understanding, the richness of this poem grows.

2. This poem consists of four quatrains rhymed *a b a b, c d c d, e f e f, g h g h*, yet the lines seem to vary in length.[4] Compare these uneven lines with the metrically even lines of William Blake's *London*. What differences do you feel from the regularity and irregularity of line?

3. What sort of man do you suppose Thomas Hardy was from the comments he has the neighbors make about him? Do you think these comments are what the neighbors will make or what the poet hopes they will make?

Two Minds

Sara Teasdale

(Page 29)

1. What does it mean to be free from "cautious human clay"?

2. What is the "zone of crystal weather / That changes not for winter or the night"? Does it sound like a good place to be?

3. There is an unconventional rhyme scheme in this poem. Write it down. The important thing is not to just notice if it is like many other poems or if it is unusual or unfamiliar, but that the poet uses the natural rhyme in words to strengthen her poem.

4. How do you feel about the words "extreme delight"? Do they express to you the feeling that these two "naked" minds must be soaring together? Or are the words too common, are they too much of a cliché?

---

[4] A *quatrain* is a four-line poem or a four-line stanza in a longer poem; a *stanza* is a number of lines fixed in the pattern of its meter and rhyme.

The Mounting Summer, Brilliant and Ominous

Delmore Schwartz

(Page 31)

1. This is an example of the kind of poem that I talked about in response to Ezra Pound's *In a Station of the Metro:* a poem painted in visual images. List 10 phrases that express a visual picture. Do you see what the poet is doing with these images? Do you get the picture? Could you paint it?

2. Look back at my response to Marianne Moore's *The Jellyfish* to refresh your memory about alliteration. Then mark two places in Schwartz's poem where he uses alliteration and tell what you think they add to the poem's effect on you.

Any Man's Advice to His Son

Kenneth Fearing

(Page 32)

1. How would you feel about your father if he gave you this advice?
   How would you feel about giving this advice to your own son?
   What does this poem say about the relationship between fathers and sons?

2. What statement does this poem make on the nature of the world?

3. Why do you agree or disagree with these two statements:
   a. "Trust no man fully."
   b. "In all this world there is nothing so easily squandered, / or once gone, so completely lost as life."

4. "If you have lost the radio beam" obviously refers to some sort of navigation. Where is the son going?

5. Read the following advice given by Polonius to his departing son Laertes (from Shakespeare's *Hamlet*). What do you think gives it its emotional power?

Polonius

Yet[5] here Laertes? Aboard, aboard, for shame;
The wind sits in the shoulder of your sail,[6]

---

[5]*yet:* still.
[6]*wind . . . sail:* the wind is favorable.

And you are stayed[7] for. There[8]—my blessing with thee.
And these few precepts in thy memory
Look thou character.[9] Give thy thoughts no tongue,[10]
Nor any unproportioned thought his act.[11]
Be thou familiar, but by no means vulgar.[12]
Those friends thou hast, and their adoption tried,[13]
Grapple them unto thy soul with hoops of steel;[14]
But do not dull thy palm with entertainment
Of each new-hatched, unfledged courage,[15] Beware
Of entrance to a quarrel, but being in,
Bear't that th' opposed[16] may beware of thee.
Give every man thy ear, but few thy voice;[17]
Take each man's censure, but reserve thy Judgement.[18]
Costly thy habit as thy purse can buy,[19]
But not expressed in fancy; rich, not gaudy,[20]
For the apparel oft proclaims the man;[21]
And they in France of the best rank and station,
Or of a most select and generous, chief in that.[22]
Neither a borrower nor a lender be,
For loan oft loses both itself and friend,
And borrowing dulleth edge of husbandry.[23]
This above all, to thine own self be true,
And it must follow, as the night the day,
Thou canst not then be false to any man.
Farewell, my blessing season[24] this in thee.

---

[7]*stayed:* waited

[8]*There:* this marks an embrace and a kiss.

[9]*these . . . character:* see that you write these precepts in your memory; *character:* write or inscribe.

[10]*Give . . . tongue:* do not say everything you think; keep your counsel.

[11]*unproportioned . . . act:* nor take a hasty, ill-considered action.

[12]*familiar:* friendly; *vulgar:* common, too easy of access.

[13]*hast . . . tried:* whose worth you have tested.

[14]*Grapple . . . steel:* stick closely and loyally to them.

[15]*dull . . . courage:* Do not make your palm callous by shaking every every man by the hand; *new-hatched:* newly made; *unfledged courage:* immature acquaintance.

[16]*Bear't that th' opposed:* carry yourself so that the opponent will be leery of you.

[17]*Give . . . voice:* listen to all but speak to few; hear more than you say.

[18]*Take . . . censure:* hear each man's opinion; *reserve thy judgement:* be reserved, cautious in your own conclusions.

[19]*Costly . . . buy:* buy the best clothes you can afford.

[20]*expressed in fancy:* conspicuous for novel style; *rich:* of fine quality; *gaudy:* flashy, vulgarly showy.

[21]*apparel . . . man:* close to the proverb "Clothes make the man."

[22]*they . . . that:* The scene is "In France the best people are renowned for such good judgement and taste in dress"; *generous:* aristocratic.

[23]*dulleth . . . husbandry:* dulls the edge of thrift.

[24]*blessing season:* may my blessing make my counsel fruitful in you.

6. Compare the advice given by Polonius to his son Laertes with the advice given by the father in Kenneth Fearing's poem. If you had a choice, which advice would you choose? What would you add or delete? Why?

I'd Want Her Eyes
to Fill with Wonder

Kenneth Patchen

(Page 33)

1. It's kind of hard to know what to ask about love poems since so many people throughout the world have written at least one during their lifetime. More songs and poems are written about love and death than any other themes. Why do you think that is true?

2. A good love song is one of the wonders of the universe. What do you think it is that makes one love song so moving and memorable while many thousands of others are so forgettable?

3. What does Kenneth Patchen mean when he uses a capital *B* in the word "beautiful"? Who "wept to see her naked loveliness"?

4. "I'd want her thighs to put birds in my fingers" is a beautiful line. What does it mean?

5. There is a refrain in this poem that Patchen had printed in italics.[25] Do you think he's trying to tell us something? How does he feel about telling her that he loves her?

Gloire de Dijon

D. H. Lawrence

(Page 35)

1. Comparing a woman to a rose is hardly a new idea in poetry, but finding new subjects is not what poetry is all about. It seems that subjects and ideas in poetry take on importance only in proportion to the greatness of the poetry. For example, in the 1960s there were thousands of songs written in protest of war. How many were hits? How many of those hit records had the lasting power to become classics (even in the limited sense of

---

[25]A *refrain* is a line that is repeated in exactly the same way.

popular music)? What makes a poem or song so powerful that it is passed on from generation to generation? If it is not the subject matter or the ideas, what is it?

2. D. H. Lawrence is a master painter. He is able to draw vivid images that pulse with life. If you were making an oil painting of the scene Lawrence describes in this poem, what colors would predominate? Why? Can you think of a famous painting that reminds you of the poem?

3. Lawrence's poetry and prose have often been criticized as being too erotic or sensual. (Look these words up in the dictionary.) Why have some given the word *sensual* negative connotations? There is a great collection of poems that has been heavily attacked throughout the past: "The Song of Solomon" from the Bible. Here is part of a love poem in Chapter 7, verses 1–3:

How beautiful are thy feet with shoes, O prince's
daughter! the joints of thy thighs are like
jewels, the work of the hands of a cunning workman.
Thy navel is like a round goblet, which wanteth not
liquor: thy belly is like an heap of wheat set
about with lilies. Thy two breasts are like two
young roes that are twins. . . .

Why do you think both this poem and Lawrence's would be the center of controversy? How did you react to them while you read them?

Gulls Land and Cease To Be
John Ciardi

(Page 37)

1. What does the title of this poem mean? When "gulls land," in what sense do they "cease to be"?

2. "the wind delicately / dumped in balance" is a surprising way of saying what?

3. Many years ago when I was in high school, I read a book by John Ciardi called *How Does a Poem Mean?* It was a poetry text which advised readers that what a poem has to say is intimately involved with the way it expresses its meaning through its shape and form. How does Ciardi shape this poem to portray the flight of the seagull? Can you see the poet shaping the poem, as a painter would shape a painting, to trace with words the flight of the gull?

4. Here is one poem where working out the rhyme scheme will tell you something about what the poet is doing. Check out the rhymes: They al-

ternate back and forth like a bird in flight until the gull lands; the poem
ends with a couplet[26] so that as the gull touches down so does the rhyme.

5. Do you think, even if these things had never occurred to you when you
   read the poem, that it would have been a good poem because it sounded
   appropriate to write about seagulls this way?

Composed upon Westminster Bridge, September 3, 1802

William Wordsworth

(Page 38)

1. This poem paints a picture of a time far different from ours. What can
   you tell about Wordsworth's London from the description in the poem?
   How might London differ today from Wordsworth's time? For a completely
   different picture of London around the same period, look at William Blake's
   poem *London*. How could two such famous poets see the same city so
   differently?

2. When I counted the rhyme scheme, I counted *a b c, a a, b b a, d e d e d e*.
   Sounds like a sonnet to me, which seems to show an irregularity in the third
   line: "majesty" does not rhyme with "fair," "by," "wear," "bare," "lie,"
   "sky," or "air." That is the kind of thing that only people who count out
   rhyme schemes ever notice, and it probably isn't very important. But there
   is something to be learned from this exercise. If we read carefully, very
   often we can see good poets using an irregularity to tell us something about
   the form or about the poem. For example, what could that break in the
   rhyme scheme emphasize in the poem?

Sonnet 76

William Shakespeare

(Page 39)

1. The poet's job is to take the old tired words that we all use every day to
   order chili dogs or lube jobs, and so forth and make them sing with a
   new sound. Hopefully, their singing will make us realize, if only for a

---

[26]Two successive lines of verse, usually in the same meter and joined by rhyme,
that form a unit.

moment, that we are alive. To what force does Shakespeare attribute the power that he brings to old words?

2. Thoreau once said that "all morality is an effort to throw off sleep," and in this sense poetry is much like Thoreau's concept of morals. What is Shakespeare telling us that he feels about the use of words?

3. Explain what the poet means by the sun being both new and old.

4. In lines 9 and 10, Shakespeare uses the word "love" to mean two different things. If you got confused there, you lost the poem. Can you explain in what two ways the word "love" is used?

5. The phrase "new pride," which ends the first line, is explained in the second line. When a poet, especially a great poet, uses a word we should look to see if he attempts to make his statement richer through *connotation* rather than just relying on the *denotation* of the word.[27]

Success Is Counted Sweetest

Emily Dickinson

(Page 41)

1. What does the poet mean by "Success is counted sweetest / By those who ne'er succeed"? What is the "purple Host"? Why is "Host" capitalized? What does the poet mean by "comprehend a nectar"? What example does Emily Dickinson give to substantiate her statement that "Success is counted sweetest / By those who ne'er succeed"?

2. Emily Dickinson's poetry is noted for containing truth and surprise. Locate the elements of truth and surprise in this poem.

---

[27]The *denotation* of a word is simply its dictionary definition, while the *connotation* of a word is anything and/or everything (in addition to the primary meaning) that we associate with it. For example, the dictionary meaning of the word "summer" is the season between spring and autumn; yet think of all the things you associate with this word—picnics, the beach, sunbathing, swimming, baseball. All in all we usually associate happy times with summer. Now think of the word "winter." You already know its denotation. What do you associate with winter? How does your connotation of this word differ from summer? Remember, a word can be like a rock thrown into a pond; it can give off ripples in all directions. When we use words, we must be aware of their connotations because they color and shape their precise meanings and sometimes change them altogether.

A Deep-Sworn Vow

William Butler Yeats

(Page 43)

1. To whom is the poet speaking?

2. What was "That deep-sworn vow"?

3. What are the states of mind Yeats refers to here, when he meets "your face"? Does that say anything about the depth of the experience described in this poem?

4. Again we find a great poet breaking the rule about not rhyming a word with itself ("face" with "face"). Why does he? Does it work? That is, does it add anything to the poem?

5. Do you think it is impossible to forget someone you once loved no matter how hard you try?

When You Are Old

William Butler Yeats

(Page 44)

1. After you read the first stanza, did you feel that Yeats was speaking directly to you? Did you imagine yourself old? If not, perhaps you should reread it.

2. Notice how the poet shifts focus. At first he could be speaking to anyone, but then he narrows his focus to one person and finally, I think, he says something about the nature of love. Mark where these shifts take place in the poem and note if they say anything to you about symmetry in poetry, about balance, about the way a good poem is made.

3. When Yeats says love "hid his face amid a crowd of stars," what does he mean?

4. Write out the rhyme scheme of this poem. Then notice how easily and simply Yeats made the formal arrangement of the poem appear effortless and natural.

5. What are the "glowing bars"? What does this relate back to in the poem? I marvel at how well constructed this poem is while appearing so natural and effortless. Do you understand what I felt?

Touch

Thom Gunn

(Page 45)

Pay careful attention to these key words: "patina," "ferment," "pogrom." Words are the tools of the poet. Consequently, if he's a good poet, he has chosen each word very carefully. When you read a poem, not knowing the meaning of a word can distort the poem for you. So always be sure that you think about the denotations and connotations of each word.

1. In the first stanza, the poet repeats three images for a state of being: "The restraint / of habits, the patina of / self, the black frost / of outsideness." Why do you think he felt it was necessary to repeat this so often?

2. What is the scene Thom Gunn presents to us? How does he give it to us? How does he broaden the horizon of the poem to include a larger idea?

3. What does the poet tell us about his lover?

4. What is the "dark / wide realm where we / walk with everyone"?

from Kaddish

Allen Ginsberg

(Page 47)

1. What things would you feel while writing a poem to your dead mother? Think of all the feelings you would have to express. Discuss some of the things Allen Ginsberg expresses as themes in his poem.

2. Define the words "Karma," "Communism," "Kaddish," "hallucinations," "mystic." First, try defining them from your own experience. How would you interpret them in a conversation? If you would say in conversation, "I don't understand that word," then use a dictionary. Notice any big differences in your definitions and the dictionary's?

3. "O Beautiful Garbo of my Karma": If you don't know who Garbo (Greta Garbo) is, ask someone over 40 or go to the library and look her up. Now, why do you think Ginsberg compared his mother to Garbo?

4. What does Ginsberg mean when he says, "Death which is the mother of the universe"? Do you know anything about the Hindu Goddess of death, Kali? If not, back to the library. Describe what this line means to you. This is important, because good poetry is not just filled with high-sounding meaningless words.

If the beautiful words do not mean anything, then it is called *pure poetry* (i.e., words orchestrated for their sound totally apart from their meaning). Perhaps this is not good poetry. But on the other hand, if we make a judgment about a poem without attempting to understand the words used, we are not being fair to the poet, to the poem, or to ourselves.

Big Momma

Don L. Lee

(Page 48)

1. Look at e. e. cumming's poetry and list the similarities and differences between his and Lee's styles of writing. Why do you think these poets used such unorthodox styles? Notice in this poem that whenever "Big Momma" speaks the lines are indented. Why did the poet do this? How does it affect your reading of the poem?

2. What is "Big Momma" referring to when she says "we never did eat too much pork / round here anyways, it was bad for the belly." Why does she think the white man doesn't have to worry about a black revolution? What is Don L. Lee saying in this poem?

3. Although "Big Momma" is never physically described, you can get a vivid picture in your mind of this wise old lady. How would you describe her?

Harsh

The Distant Drum

Calvin C. Hernton

(Page 53)

1. What is Calvin Hernton telling us?

2. List some metaphors and symbols that he uses to get his message across. A *metaphor* makes a comparison between two things, thereby making us see one or both in a new way. A *symbol* is a word or image for something that implies something much larger; for example, the cross is a symbol in our culture for Christianity, but it also represents many other things.

3. In case you did not touch on this, why does the poet begin by saying that he is neither a "metaphor" nor a "symbol"?

4. What does this poem tell us about one role the poet can play in men's lives? In other words, what can the poet do in his society to affect men's lives? How? What is this poet doing?

Santa Claus

Howard Nemerov

(Page 54)

1. First the words: What do "inverted," "soupçon," "sycophant," and "parable" mean?

2. What does the poet mean when he says "His bloated Other"?

3. Do you think the poet is concerned with putting "Christ back in Christmas," as the posters advise? Could he be using the Christian myth[28] to point up the hypocrisy of our society in claiming to be "Christian" while using this myth for the shabby practice of selling shoddy goods?

4. The way the poem is divided into stanzas is appropriate to the motion of the poem. What shifts in approach characterize the three stanzas? How are they different from each other in what they tell us about Santa Claus?

5. The basic conflict here is between the material and the spiritual. Is one better than the other in the poet's mind, or is it a conflict of honesty versus dishonesty?

---

[28]The stories and characters of a people or culture, usually as related to their historic past or early origins. Ancient religions (e.g., Greeks and Romans) used them to tell the stories of their gods and goddesses.

Wisdom

Sara Teasdale

(Page 55)

1. One of the greatest pleasures I've had in working on this book is dealing with the work of Sara Teasdale. The beauty of her poetry is that she is able to express complete ideas with simple language. It was unnecessary to keep a dictionary at your side while you read this poem. How did this affect your reading?

2. Try to paraphrase what the poet is saying. Then put what you have written side by side with her poem. Which is more lucid, more memorable, more powerful? Why?

3. What is the rhyme scheme of this poem? Try writing eight lines using the same pattern of rhymes (though not necessarily the same rhymes or the same words). Compare your poem with hers.

4. What does the poet mean by "the Truth"? Why does this new knowledge take away her youth? What do you associate with youth?

5. The poem's first lines talk about wings breaking. What did you visualize when you read these lines? How did the image help you understand the poem?

Africa's Plea

Roland Tombekai Dempster

(Page 57)

1. The two words most often used here are *you* and *me*. Over and over again they play off each other. What is there about this poem that makes that seem appropriate? In other words, does the subject of this poem lend itself to the repetition of *you, me?*

2. Discuss the political situation described.

3. Could you look at this poem as a personal plea from black people for black cultural freedom anywhere? If so, what is the subject of this poem?

London

William Blake

(Page 58)

1. Blake was an engraver and his books were often illustrated with his own visual art. This poem was originally illustrated with two scenes. One scene showed a young boy leading an old, bearded, white-haired man through the streets of London; the other showed a young street urchin warming himself by a fire. Both were intended to depict the squalor of industrialized London. Describe the picture Blake paints with words. How is this picture different from the one William Wordsworth described in *Composed upon West-minster Bridge, September 3, 1802?*

2. I will not ask you to guess what "charter'd" means as applied to the street and the Thames. It refers to the restricting effects of the charters and cor-porations on the individual and sets the tone of a political poem. What are some of the other political and social comments made in this poem?

3. "mind-forg'd manacles" describes beautifully a state of mind Blake detested and of which he was remarkably free. He once wrote of himself:

   The angel that presided over my birth
   Said little creature formed of joy and mirth
   Go love without the help of any king on earth.

   Can you see why this sort of a person would be sensitive to the ugliness of an industrializing London (around 1810)? Give some contemporary ex-amples of this sort of a person. How about including some poets?

4. Can you sort out what Blake is saying about marriage and harlots and infants and hearses?

Hello

Robert Creeley

(Page 59)

1. Have you ever had a poem come off the page and hook you before? Did it happen with this one?

2. Describe how Creeley made the imagery so vivid.

3. Why do you think this sort of poem could not have been written until the middle of the twentieth century? What could have caused this to happen naturally now and not at an earlier time in history?

4. Compare this poem with others we have read. How is this one different? What effect does the poet seek to have on us?

Impasse

Langston Hughes

(Page 61)

I once found an old newspaper clipping at the bottom drawer of an elderly woman's pile of junk at the flea market. It had a recipe on one side and on the other, part of a story about the "Negro poet Langston Hughes" being refused permission to use the auditorium at Palo Alto High School to give a reading. The article was cut off where the recipe ended so I don't know the outcome or the reason given (I can guess), nor do I know the date. But this struggle has been going on for a long time, and Langston Hughes took his honorable place in it early and spoke (still speaks) strongly, and plainly, and directly to the problem—does anyone really care?

1. This has an interesting rhyme scheme. What allows the "am"–"damn" rhyme to come across so strongly, even though the words are four lines apart?

A Bill to My Father

Edward Field

(Page 62)

1. When we look at one sort of behavior pattern and attempt to see how it should be applied in another context, we often learn something about both spheres of life. Here business and the family crisscross. How is the poet expressing his resentment of his father? Does he also seem to resent the world of business? What comment does the poem make about identity? About fairness?

2. Does the last line make the poem work? How?

3. Alienation is a major theme that runs throughout many contemporary poems, movies, novels, short stories, and plays. Why can't we communicate with each other? Why don't people know how to show their love? What do they fear? Are you afraid to show your love? Why?

4. Why are fathers and sons afraid, after a certain age, to demonstrate and verbalize their love for each other? Is this true in all cultures or nations?

Jealousy
Rupert Brooke

(Page 63)

1. The themes of sickness and decay emerge from this poem and seem to be expressed out of hate. Describe the picture that Brooke paints of the wife's future.

2. What is happening in the poet's life (if he is writing about himself)? What causes this flood of ugliness and hate? Does he dramatize the emotion vividly enough for you? Does this strike you as an accurate portrait of an ugly emotion?

3. Did you notice that this modern poem about a contemporary subject is written in couplets? Can you give any reason why the poet chose to write in couplets?

4. List some ways in which this poem gains its power.

5. Compare this poem to *A Bill to My Father*. Which do you feel depicts the emotion of the poet better (i.e., in a stronger, more memorable way)?

A Teacher
Reed Whittemore

(Page 64)

1. This is another poem that paints a picture of a human condition. What did the teacher think of his students? Describe the attitude with which he approached his life.

2. "Gladly would he learn and gladly teach" is a famous line from the prologue of Chaucer's *The Canterbury Tales*. What added dimension can it give a poem to share a line with a well-known story? How can this make it richer for the sympathetic reader (not just the character who gets off on the fact that he knows the reference)? In what ways does this make a poem bigger, more memorable, better?

3. Who is Babbitt? Look it up in your dictionary, but for a really complete picture go to the library and look it up in a literary reference book such as *The Reader's Encyclopedia*.

4. From the way the teacher is depicted here, does he have anything worth teaching?

5. In the lines "Mercantile Main Street Babbitt / Bourgeois-barbaric faces," we have a special use of sound called *alliteration*. How does this use of sound influence the poem?

Five Ways to Kill a Man

Edwin Brock

(Page 65)

1. What are the five ways to kill a man described here? What does the fifth way imply?

It seems to me that the quality of this poem depends on how tellingly the poet describes each event and how powerfully he presents the four historical pictures and the contemporary view. I ask that you be a critic here. To me criticism is a much less important skill than the ability to enjoy a work of art; I prefer the response of pleasure to the response of praise. But we all make judgments about things, which leads us to look for standards by which we can measure them. That's okay; we all do it naturally. There's no use saying, "I'll not do it." But I think we can say, "I'll attempt to do it well. I'll attempt to find for myself what makes a thing good and praise that while criticizing what makes something less good." But we miss the point entirely if we get too wrapped up in analysis and lose sight of the fact that poetry is pleasure for the ear and food for the soul.

2. Now then, do you think this poem makes it according to your standards. Why or why not?

The Golf Links Lie So Near the Mill

Sarah N. Cleghorn

(Page 67)

The social problem of child labor is the focus of this quatrain. At one time in the history of our country, this was the cause célèbre, the social issue of the nineteenth and early twentieth centuries. The protest continued until suitable laws were enacted to prevent children from being abused by industry. (See the novels of Charles Dickens on the problem in England, those of Sinclair Lewis in America, and see the photography of Lewis Hine.) Hundreds of books were written about the issue—from well-thought-out arguments to hysterical tracts.

1. Why has this little quatrain survived when so many of the volumes written are gathering moths in the basements of public libraries?

2. Although over one hundred years separate the writing of William Blake's poem, London, and Cleghorn's poem, The Golf Links Lie So Near the Mill, both poems were written to protest social conditions. Reread both poems and then discuss how each poet's choice of words affects the imagery.

Discovery

Hilaire Belloc

(Page 68)

1. What has the poet discovered?

2. Compare this poem with Sara Teasdale's *Wisdom*. Would the two poets have much in common? What do the two poems have in common in the way they are structured?

3. What percentage of people in our culture do you think make the discoveries outlined in this poem without the foresight of poetry? Could the wisdom discussed in the poem be called "conventional wisdom"? Is this the kind of understanding that a conventional American businessman would want to be able to pass on to his son (the wisdom of not how to excel, but how to get by)?

True Love at Last

D. H. Lawrence

(Page 69)

1. Finding a book of D. H. Lawrence poems the summer I turned 16 changed my life. I decided "if this is poetry, I dig poetry." Before then, I had never related to the poems I had been tested on in school. But Lawrence was talking about something I wanted to understand: life. What is he saying to you here about love? The line "I must see if I can't absorb this Samson of self-absorption" contains some alliteration again. What is the historical reference to Samson?

2. Lawrence wrote many short stories, poems, plays, essays, and novels. Throughout his writing, he stated that the principal conflict in human beings is between their need to preserve themselves as complete, independent individuals and their need to relate themselves in some way to the whole of creation: to other people, to animals, to the sun and the stars. Consequently, he often wrote a great deal about the conflict between the sexes and how, in the adjustment of the sexes to each other, this conflict reached its most dramatic proportions. Do you see this conflict in the poem?

3. It has often been said that in every love relationship one of the partners must dominate the other. Do you agree or disagree with this idea? Discuss.

In the Convalescent Hospital

Jean Pumphrey

(Page 70)

1. Describe the speaker of this poem. Is she the poet? Who is she then?

2. What does the reference to "Christ" mean? Discuss the two references to "cages." What "cage" is the old woman in? What is "your cage of flesh"? What comment does she make by putting the two together?

3. Discuss how the poet looks at death in this poem; then describe the feeling *you* get. Would you say that the poet is attempting to make a case for euthanasia, or is she asking what I consider the basic question: What is the meaning of life?

4. Does the poet lead you to ask some questions with her? What are they?

5. Since we've got our critical approaches warmed up, I'll say that I think this is a good poem. Agree? Disagree? Why?

I Shall Not Care

Sara Teasdale

(Page 71)

1. Sara Teasdale, wife of a St. Louis businessman, committed suicide in 1933. What attitude does this poem express about life? Does it constitute a suicide note?

2. What sort of person would take the pains to write so lovingly about his or her own death? Don't even try to answer that; it was more a question I was asking myself upon reading "and over me bright April / Shakes out her rain-drenched hair." It seems Sara Teasdale had one foot firmly planted in the mud of life even while she contemplated her own death.

3. To whom do you think the poem is directed? Why?

4. Write down the rhyme scheme. It's amazing to me how often the most powerful poems are so simple in structure.

Tomorrow, and Tomorrow, and Tomorrow

William Shakespeare

(Page 73)

If I were hearing this poem for the first time, I'd find a copy of *Macbeth* and turn to act 5 to read it in its dramatic context.

1. What's happening to Macbeth that he should feel this way about life? If judged by the number of people who quote these lines, many of us must have shared the emotion at some time in our lives.

2. When a person feels this way about life, is it truth he has discovered or his own personal emptiness and failure?

3. Calling life a "brief candle" is a metaphor. List three other metaphors in this poem. What color does each add to the basic subject, "Life is like . . ."? In other words, what does Shakespeare tell us about how Macbeth *feels* by using metaphoric examples?

4. Read this over 10 times, 100 times. Read the whole act, read the whole play. Play the recording of the play over and over. Shakespeare is better equipped to tell you about himself than any teacher. And the more familiar you are with his plays, the more sense you will get out of what teachers do say about them.

American Rhapsody (2)

Kenneth Fearing

(Page 74)

1. This poem seems to deal with projections into the future: "first you . . . then you . . . then you. . . ." What direction do events take, toward the better or the worse?

2. What is a rhapsody? What does the title add to the poem?

3. Look at how many things the poet has organized in groups of three and four. Do you get into the rhythm of that? Does it help you feel the emotion the poet is working to get across? Describe how this repetition works on you.

4. Does this poem *give you the feeling* of how easy it is to allow our dreams and ideals to be submerged in the tedium of daily existence? Is this a poem rather than a statement of some fact or theory? Does it create some emotion in you? Besides the repetition, how does the poet accomplish this? Describe the effect.

For Saundra

Nikki Giovanni

(Page 75)

1. What are the questions the poet explores about poetry? About the state of the nation?

Nature seems to be used as a metaphor here: the state of the trees is like the state of Manhattan, and the state of the clouds is like the state of our country "since no-Dick was elected." If you read this poem with your eyes and ears open, even if you don't stop and think about it, you will get a feeling from this picture that compares no trees and clouds with the drab asphalt urban blight and the election of Richard Nixon. To become conscious of this, read the poem again and see if this drawing together of things influences your feeling. That's what metaphor is all about. It is the bringing together of two things by showing they are similar in some way and intertwining them so that the way we see both of them is changed.

2. The poet is saying that there is a time for writing and a time for fighting and that now might be the time for fighting; and yet from this discussion we are given not violence, but this poem. How does that strike you? What does that say to you about the nature of poetry?

3. When in history have there ever been poetic times? Men sing in all times, and often the great ages of poetry have been but brief respites between battles.

Hour of Concern

Lindley Williams Hubbell

(Page 76)

1. If Lindley Hubbell is trying to say that people prefer trivia and gossip to dealing with real problems, he does a pretty good job. Did you get the references? Who is Ingrid Bergman? What is a Stromboli sandwich? A Stromboli cocktail?

2. In conversation an individual can indicate his mood and attitude through his tone of voice, inflection, pitch, and emphasis. He can also use facial expressions and gestures. In poetry, *tone* refers to the attitude of the poet toward his subject, his audience, and himself. What is the poet's tone in this poem? What words, phrasing, or lines reveal this to you?

New Approach Needed

Kingsley Amis

(Page 77)

Poets and other writers often use a style of writing in which the speaker, in a particular situation, addresses one or more silent listeners, revealing his private thoughts and emotions. It is called a *dramatic monologue*. Robert Browning, a famous twentieth-century poet, frequently used this technique in his poetry.

1. In this poem, to whom is the speaker talking?

2. What is he criticizing? Do you agree with him?

Dear America

Robert Peterson

(Page 79)

1. You could say that this is an *epistle* (a letter in verse) written to America. Describe the feelings expressed.

2. Does the poet seem to be writing to make the reader feel something in a certain way or is he writing to express his own feelings?

3. "Who are you to ask me to be a statistic / or a lizard?" With what qualities of the lizard is Peterson suggesting we associate metaphorically with America's demands on him?

4. Relate the feelings expressed here to the situation described in Vachel Lindsay's *The Leaden-Eyed*.

5. Using your own critical standards, which do you think is the stronger poem? Why?

Poem to a Nigger Cop

Bobb Hamilton

(Page 80)

1. This poem is addressed to some basic issues. What are the main ones? How real do you think the conflicts are?

2. A *simile* makes a comparison between two things the same as a metaphor

does, except that it is more direct and uses the words "like" or "as." For example: "Your teeth rolling across the screen / Like undotted dice." What is being compared here? Can you visualize it?

Similes are easy to identify because they make comparisons with the help of "like" or "as." Metaphors are less easy to spot because they omit these connective words while making the same sort of comparison with more subtlety.

3. Find a metaphor in this poem.

Mourn Not the Dead

Ralph Chaplin

(Page 81)

1. In each stanza the poet comments on a specific type of individual. Can you identify each type? Do you agree with Chaplin's conclusion about "the apathetic throng"? Why or why not?

2. Relate this poet's feelings about the mass of people. Now look at Vachel Lindsay's poem *The Leaden-Eyed*. Critically judge Ralph Chaplin's poem and compare. Which do you think is better? Why?

The Leaden-Eyed

Vachel Lindsay

(Page 83)

1. What is Vachel Lindsay crying out for in this poem? What disturbs him?

2. Chart the rhyme scheme. It fascinates me that something so powerful arranged in such a basic pattern of rhyme, can be fashioned from words we all use. Do you see how rhyme gives emphasis here to increase the power of the words?

3. What are "quaint deeds"?

4. I suggest that you write a quatrain rhymed *a b c b*. Write about anything—baseball, rock stars, geology, anything—but work on it until the lines flow like these do. You do not have to spend two months on this: just long enough to get the idea of how much work is involved in writing well. If you care about your writing, you could not do anything more important that would help you more as a poet.

American Primitive

William Jay Smith

(Page 84)

1. To what does the title refer? Does it refer to a style of art in which the father is depicted in a painting on the wall, or to the sort of person the father must be? Or both? That is one of the rich things about dealing with the emotions. When the intellect says "this" or "that" constitutes a choice, you can't have both. But the emotions deal with unclear things that confuse the mind. We must educate our emotions to accept this richness, for the intellect will make unnecessary choices and cut us off from many good possibilities.

2. In life it is possible for two different things to be true, and often we must accept *both* to see an honest picture. Is that what is happening in *American Primitive?*

3. What does the refrain "I love my Daddy like he loves his dollar" mean?

Mothers, Daughters

Shirley Kaufman

(Page 85)

1. The poet expresses very clearly and powerfully the emotions a mother feels toward her daughter. What makes this a poem? Why is this more than a clear expression of powerful feelings?

2. "She's cruel, / as if my private meanness / found a way to punish us": Briefly describe the emotions expressed by the mother here. Do you think these are common or even normal feelings, or does the poet lead you to think they are weird or even criminal?

3. How old is the daughter? How did you reach your conclusion?

Daddy

Sylvia Plath

(Page 86)

1. Be sure to read this poem out loud. There is a lot going on by way of phantasmagoric autobiography and the use of language.[29] First, sort out the life of the woman as presented in the poem. If you feel close to this poem, look up the life of Sylvia Plath and see how it relates to the things represented.

2. Is the poet speaking of psychological poetic facts or actual facts in the events described here? If you do not know from research, what do you feel from the words of the poem? Why?

3. Listen carefully, hear what the poet is doing with the sound of language.

---

[29]A *phantasmagoric autobiography* is an account of a person's life written by himself and filled with a shifting series of phantasms, illusions, or deceptive appearances as in a dream or as created by the imagination.

Light

Introduction to *Songs of Innocence*

William Blake

(Page 91)

1. We have already read one poem by William Blake (*London*) that deals with a serious social problem. We see another aspect of the poet in the introductory poem to *Songs of Innocence*. Blake published two sets of poems together and called them *Songs of Innocence* and *Songs of Experience; London* is in the latter. From the two examples, can you say how these two sets of poems would fit together to make one statement? What do you think the statement is?

2. William Blake died in bed in 1827, at the age of 70, singing hymns of praise to God. Notice the simplicity and directness of the language and the form of the songs. Does the form match the message?

3. What is happening in the poem? What event is the poet describing?

The Perforated Spirit

Morris Bishop

(Page 92)

1. Compare the structure[30] of this poem to Sylvia Plath's *Daddy*. Describe the attitude of the poet to the situation he describes. How do you feel about the situation? Have you ever shared the poet's attitude? What gives Morris Bishop's poem its humor and power?

2. "The files are masters of my fate, / They are captains of my soul" resonates in our ears because it contains an allusion we have all heard but may not remember specifically.[31] The lines refer to a famous poem written by the English poet William Ernest Henley (1849–1903) entitled *Invictus*. Its last lines read:

> It matters not how strait the gate
> How charged with punishment the scroll,
> I am the master of my fate,
> I am the captain of my soul.

---

[30]Structure refers to the arrangement of the larger part of a literary work. It also refers to the total work, to the complex interaction of all the various materials that shape a poem.

[31]An *allusion* is a reference to a person, place, or occurrence in religion, mythology, history, or literature.

3. Henley wrote this poem while he was a patient in a tuberculosis hospital. *Invictus* is the Latin word for unconquered. Children for the past 75 years or so have been forced to memorize these lines. Compare the feeling expressed in *The Perforated Spirit* to that contained in Henley's poem. John Ciardi, famous contemporary poet, author, and editor, has called *Invictus* the most widely known bad poem in English. Do you agree with him?

An Elegy on the Death of a Mad Dog

Oliver Goldsmith

(Page 93)

1. Again, please take note of the structure. Do you have any observations on how one structural form could be put to such diverse uses?

2. What is an *elegy?*

3. Oliver Goldsmith's attitude toward the man was filled with ironic over-tones.[32] What does the conclusion tell you about what preceded it? When did you begin to catch on that Goldsmith wasn't being straightforward?

4. The key question is one of appearance versus reality or "Why aren't things what they seem?" Why do you think that question makes us laugh?

The Naming of Cats

T. S. Eliot

(Page 95)

1. Why does T. S. Eliot think the naming of cats is a difficult matter? What reasons does he give for the three different types of names?

2. Look up Plato, Admetus, Electra, and Demeter. What is a "quorum"? What does "ineffable" mean?

3. What is the tone of the poem? Do you think T. S. Eliot understands cats? Why?

---

[32]*Irony* means saying one thing while meaning another in order to mock someone or something.

The Story of My Life

Hollis Summers

(Page 97)

1. Be sure to pay attention to the words used in this poem since much of the humor revolves around the poet's choice of words. What does "sylphs," "paradigm," and "cavilling" mean?

2. Why is hindsight easier than foresight? (Use your dictionary for these definitions.) The generation gap between you and your parents seems to close once *you* reach 30. Why?

3. This poem is humorous because it contains an ironic ending. Were you surprised by it?

Grim Fairy Tale

Lionel Wiggam

(Page 98)

1. Write out the rhyme scheme for this poem. Is it different from the other poems you have studied? How?

2. What fairy tale is the basis for this poem? Describe what transpires. How does the poet's use of language make the poem amusing? The title of this poem contains an allusion. What is it? The title also contains a double meaning. Did you catch it?

The Frog Prince

Robert Pack

(Page 99)

1. This poem is based on the same fairy tale as *Grim Fairy Tale,* but it goes off in a different direction. Which do you prefer? Which do you think is a better poem? Why?

2. At what line does the poet begin to let you know what is coming? Can you answer the question asked in the last line of the poem: "What was it that her mother said?"

For Anne Gregory

William Butler Yeats

(Page 101)

1. Each of the stanzas in this poem constitutes a conversation. Reread the poem. Which stanza or stanzas contain Anne Gregory's dialogue? Once you discover this, how does it change your insights into the poem?

2. What are "great honey-coloured / Ramparts"? In this poem a man is attempting to communicate something to a woman. What is Yeats saying to Anne Gregory?

3. There is a kind of overstatement, or hyperbole, used here.[33] Consequently, can we take the words of the poet literally? How does Yeats let us know that he means something a little different?

You will recall that a line which recurs at the end of each stanza is called a *refrain*. I encourage you to learn poetic terms because sometimes knowing the right word makes talking about poems so much more meaningful. Sometimes something a poet writes does not become clear unless we understand some concept or tradition. There are many good literature terminology handbooks available in inexpensive paperback editions. They're awfully good to have handy.

Jabberwocky

Lewis Carroll

(Page 102)

Lewis Carroll (1832–1898) was a minister who taught mathematics and in his spare time entertained children.[34] He once said, "I like all children so long as they are girls." He originally wrote *Alice in Wonderland* and *Through the Looking Glass* to amuse the children of Dean Liddell of Christ Church, Oxford; but they later became enormously popular among adult readers. He also produced a fine book of photographic portraits of Victorian children (girls) and many poems.

I am not going to ask you what this poem means, although if you went to the library you could read some incredible accounts of the different meanings readers have gotten from it. Just read this poem aloud and enjoy it.

1. If you want a question to answer, list some of the words we hear from time to time that Lewis Carroll made up in this poem.

---

[33]A *hyperbole* is an exaggeration or extravagance in statement for the purpose of giving an effect.
[34]Lewis Carroll is the pseudonym of Charles Lutwidge Dodgson.

As I said earlier, there is a kind of writing called *pure poetry,* which is poetry written for the sake of its music and images; it is meant to be appreciated for that alone. If you come across a lovely passage and cannot figure out what it means, maybe it doesn't have a meaning you can translate into intellectual terms (e.g., "OBLA Di, OBLA Da").

In *Through the Looking Glass,* Lewis Carroll assists those who insist on knowing the meaning of words by having Humpty Dumpty explain to Alice that

> . . . "slithy" means "lithe and slimy"
> "Lithe" is the same as active. You see
> it's like a portmanteau—there are two
> meanings packed up in one word.

Humpty Dumpty also identified "mimsy" as another portmanteau word made up of "flimsy" and "miserable."[35]

Song of the Open Road

Ogden Nash

(Page 103)

Ogden Nash is famous for his light verse. It is usually written in long, rambling, ill-balanced couplets; no attempt at meter; and it contains strained or oversimplified rhymes, in a burlesque of inferior poetry.[36] This short, amusing verse is a parody of the very famous poem *Trees* by Alfred Joyce Kilmer.[37] Read Kilmer's poem.

Trees

For Mrs. Henry Mills Alden

I think that I shall never see
A poem lovely as a tree.

A tree whose hungry mouth is prest
Against the earth's sweet, flowing breast;

A tree that may in Summer wear
A nest of robins in her hair;

Upon whose bosom snow has lain;
Who intimately lives with rain.

Poems are made by fools like me.
But only God can make a tree.

Alfred Joyce Kilmer

---

[35] A *portmanteau* is an artificial word made up of parts of other words and is expressive of a combination denoted by those parts.

[36] A *burlesque* is a humorous imitation of a serious piece of literature or writing.

[37] A *parody* is a satirical imitation of a novel or poem.

1. Now do you see why Ogden Nash made fun of it? In the not too distant past, generations of schoolchildren were required to memorize this poem. How does Kilmer's poem differ from the contemporary poems included in this anthology? Which do you prefer? Why?

2. *Trees* contains a great deal of personification.[38] Locate some examples of this type of figurative language.

Dr. Fatt, Instructor

Donald Hall

(Page 104)

1. What sort of person is Dr. Fatt? How do the lines quoting Dr. Fatt on Shakespeare's plays show his attitude toward his students?

2. What is Donald Hall saying about school administrators? About some college professors? Do you agree with the poet? Why or why not? Have you ever had such a teacher?

3. How does the title of the poem relate to the line "He waddles brilliantly from class to class"?

Sometime During Eternity

Lawrence Ferlinghetti

(Page 105)

1. *Free verse* is verse written in a form that does not obey the rules for metrical verse (words written in a specific, formally organized pattern). Free verse is still a "form," that is, a way of organizing writing and experience. But instead of using stiff traditional patterns, the poet depends on such devices as assonance, alliteration, and cadence.[39] Can you see the form used by Lawrence Ferlinghetti? Can you see a pattern in his use of language?

---

[38]*Personification* is the attribution of human characteristics to an inanimate object or abstract idea.

[39]*Cadence* is the beat of any rhythmical movement. *Assonance* is a peculiar form of rhyme in which the last accented vowel sounds and succeeding vowels, if any, must be identical.

2. What is the effect of discussing Jesus in the term the poet uses? What effect do they have on your feelings toward Christ? Amplify what Ferlinghetti is saying.

3. Compare the New Testament version of the crucifixion with Ferlinghetti's version. Why does he put a capital on "Petered out"?

The Dover Bitch:
A Criticism of Life

Anthony Hecht

(Page 107)

Like many things in literature, this poem refers to another and more famous poem—*Dover Beach* by Matthew Arnold. Anthony Hecht's poem is a parody of it. But before you begin any questions or discussion, read both poems.

1. In one or two sentences, state the theme of *Dover Beach*. Now do the same same thing for *The Dover Bitch*.

2. What sort of person is the Dover Bitch? Is she common in your world? What does Hecht imply is wrong with her? What is "Nuit d'Amour"? How do you think women's liberation would react to this poem? Why?

3. Try to write a parody of a famous poem. Do not be discouraged at first to find it isn't easy; since it takes a great deal of practice to be skilled at writing with humor.

President Langton

Daniel J. Langton

(Page 109)

1. What is the role of personal fantasy in poetry? What is the role of fantasy in our everyday life?

2. Is this poem an implied criticism of the actualities of the presidency? If so, how?

3. What attitudes toward the presidency does the poet find attractive?

4. Do you think Langton would be a good president? Why?

Second Fig
Edna St. Vincent Millay

(Page 111)

1. How would you characterize the two realtors contrasted here? Essentially what two worlds are being compared?

2. Write a closed couplet.[40] In other words, write a two-line poem much like this one. Try to make some statement about two concepts.

American Gothic
To Satch

Samuel Allen
(Paul Vesey)

(Page 112)

1. Would this poem make sense to you if you did not know who Satch is? Could you figure it out?

2. Describe the feeling expressed. Does the language involve you in this feeling? How?

Underwear
Lawrence Ferlinghetti

(Page 113)

1. This poem is written in free verse, which was commonly used by a great many twentieth-century poets. Walt Whitman used it in the nineteenth century, and his work heavily influenced later American poets, particularly in the 1920s and 1930s.

2. Could this poem be called a burlesque? At what things is the poet poking fun?

3. There are many literary references (allusions) in this poem. Locate as many as you can. Can you still enjoy the poem without recognizing all of them?

---

[40]A *closed* couplet is one in which the sense is completed within the two lines.

The Purist

Ogden Nash

(Page 116)

1. Compare the tone of this poem to that expressed in Donald Hall's poem *Dr. Fatt*. Do they sound much the same to you? In what ways? (Look at the way Ogden Nash controls language to express his attitude.)

2. What sort of person is Nash poking fun at here? What is a purist? Have you ever met one? Describe him or her.

Telephone Conversation

Wole Soyinka

(Page 117)

1. This poet has a clever way of making a statement (the last two lines of the poem). What is the statement and how does he go about making it so cleverly?

2. Notice the wonderful names given to colors. They make you see them, taste them, and smell them. That is one good way of charging language with music. If you care about your own ability to express yourself in a powerful, memorable way, jot down some words that make colors come alive for you.

3. In a sentence or so describe the scene that occurred here.

The Bride of Frankenstein

Edward Field

(Page 118)

1. Although this poem contains a great deal of humor, it makes several serious comments about the human condition. What comment is the poet making about beauty queens when the bride of Frankenstein begins "to understand that in this life too / she was just another body to be raped"? Would women's liberation agree with him? Why?

2. What is the tone of the poem?

3. This poem contains several notable examples of onomatopoeia.[41] Can you locate them?

---

[41]*Onomatopoeia* is the use of words whose sound imitates the things they name, for example, "buzz," "hiss."

The Plot to Assassinate
the Chase Manhattan Bank

Carl Larsen

(Page 121)

1. There are a lot of allusions in this poem. Did you make the connections? For example: "Love, In God We trust," "Jean Valjean," "Kings-X," "rainbow doves," "The Proletariat demands," "the Bronx." Each refers to something. What? Ask your reference librarian to help you. What do each of these allusions make us picture?
2. In a few sentences, describe the view of deceit presented here.
3. According to the poet, what is society missing?
4. Is the poet "crazy"? Or is it a sign of sanity to turn such madness into poems rather than headlines?

The Rebel

Mari E. Evans

(Page 123)

This poem is called a *fourteener*.[42] This brings up the question: Why write in forms at all? Everyone who thinks about poetry at all asks this question. My answer is vague, but there is something in the human mind that seeks to impose order (patterns) on the randomness of experience. The mind does this naturally. We make lists of things to do. We sing songs, and the ones that rhyme or have distinctive sounds are easier to remember so we sing them the most and, consequently, more people hear and eventually sing them. From this, fixed forms evolve. (The sonnet is one example, but across the world there are hundreds of fixed forms with X number of lines rhymed in such and such an order with so many sounds per line, etc.)

The forms that lend themselves to poetic expression become part of tradition and therefore part of the educational system of a culture. Why do poets use them? Probably to see if they can. They are a real challenge. If you want to understand why, pick one of the fixed forms (e.g., the sonnet, p. 13, or the villanelle,[43] p. 168) and write one. You don't have to bare your soul for this one; just see if you can make the words fit. If it seems too archaic (or anything else you don't relate to), take the music of a popular song and write new words. Good Luck!

---

[42]A *fourteener* is an iambic line of fourteen syllables or seven feet.

[43]A *villanelle* is a poem of five three-line stanzas followed by a quatrain and having only two rhymes. In the stanzas following the first, the first and third lines of the first stanza are repeated in alternation as refrains. They are the final two lines of the concluding quatrain.

The Artist
William Carlos Williams
(Page 124)

1. What is an "entrechat"?

2. William Carlos Williams once again photographs an experience with words. Describe this scene.

3. The poem ends with the question, "What goes on here?" Could the poet be asking the same question of us all? In other words, immediacy—the now, now, now—may be what the poet is talking about. If you understand that, explain how he is attempting to communicate with us about immediacy.

Horror Movie
Howard Moss
(Page 125)

1. Howard Moss is burlesquing all horror movies. Do you readily recognize each beloved movie monster? Why do audiences enjoy horror movies so much? Does this reveal something about man's basic nature? The poet makes a statement in the last lines of the poem. Does this answer the above two questions? Do you agree with the statement?

2. In order to thoroughly enjoy this poem, you *must* read it and recognize the poet's tone. What is it?

3. The rhyme scheme is very simple: Only a skilled craftsman can create such a poem without sounding corny. Part of the humor of this poem lies in its dreadful rhyme scheme.

The Origin of Baseball
Kenneth Patchen
(Page 127)

1. Who are General Sherman and Elizabeth Barrett Browning?

2. If you like this poem, find books by Kenneth Patchen and read them from cover to cover. He has written thousands of poems using his mixture of

whimsy and gentleness. If imagination is part of what *art* is all about, Kenneth Patchen should be remembered for a long time to come.

3. Describe what this poem is about.

4. "Time, . . . what's / That mean—time?" What comment is the poet making about the relationship of the world to time? Relate this to the William Carlos Williams poem *The Artist*.

An Easy Decision

Kenneth Patchen

(Page 128)

1. What a beautiful man Kenneth Patchen was. What did he decide here? What was the basis for his decision? How do the words of the poem emphasize this?

2. Why does modern man need fantasy in his life? What other famous writers use fantasy?

she being Brand

e. e. cummings

(Page 129)

1. e. e. cumming's works often combine lyricism, humor (frequently bawdy), satire, typographical experiment, unabashed sex, and the wonder and innocence of childhood. Once you unlock his unconventional style, the rhythm and imagery of his poetry are sheer joy.

2. How does cummings use punctuation, spelling, word spacing, and the like to help him tell his story? What precisely is the poem about?

3. How does using the pronouns "she" and "her" increase the double meaning of the poem?

Love Song

Dorothy Parker

(Page 131)

Dorothy Parker was noted for her caustic sense of humor, and many of her poems deal with the abrasive relationships that can exist between men and women.

1. We've all heard hundreds of poems like this, written (not so skillfully) by high school imitators of Elizabethan poets. But in this poem, the eighth line of each stanza turns everything around. What effect does it have to build up with sentimental clichés only to smash through with bitterness and cynicism? How does this affect you?

A Sane Revolution

D. H. Lawrence

(Page 133)

1. What is Lawrence advocating? Do you think it is a good idea? Is it possible to have a "sane" revolution? Discuss.

God and Man

Samuel Hazo

(Page 134)

1. What do you think of this as a description of the state of man?

2. The stage is a common metaphor for life. In this poem, to what story does this metaphor refer?

3. Look at Shakespeare's poem *Tomorrow, and Tomorrow, and Tomorrow.* The stage is also used as a metaphor in it. How did the two poets make the same metaphor work so differently?

4. What does the poet mean by "the female lead blundered on page / one"?

God Is Mr. Big, Real Big

Carl F. Burke

(Page 135)

1. Get a copy of the Bible and read Exodus 20:3–17. Notice how the poet has changed the original version of the Ten Commandments. Would you call this poem a parody? Why?

2. Some purists would not consider this a poem because it is written in an unconventional style and relies heavily on free verse. How do you react to this style of writing? Do you like it? Why?

Heavy

When The Ripe Fruit Falls

D. H. Lawrence

(Page 139)

1. David Herbert Lawrence is noted for his fantastic word pictures about nature. His novels and poems are filled with the color, intensity of feeling, and mysticism he associated with nature. He believed that man's attitudes toward nature were deeply associated with his attitudes toward human good, human destiny, human happiness, human salvation, and the characteristic problems of being human. How does this information relate to the poem?

2. What does "distils" mean? Literally? Metaphorically? Where does the word "chaos" come from? What is a "fulfilled" person? How could such a person be compared to "ripe fruit"?

3. Paraphrase this poem, that is, restate the poem in other words. What is left out? Describe what was lost when you put the poem into the loose language of your prose.

4. Trace the image of "oil" through the poem. How does it hold the poem together?

To Look at Any Thing

John Moffitt

(Page 141)

1. This poem, if we hear it, brings us into contact with *essence:* the very core, the very central issue of being alive. What is the poet asking us to do?

2. Why will the traditional response "I have seen spring in these woods" not do? What more is expected?

3. What method does the poet use to put us in touch with deeper realities?

4. Describe a picture (painting, photograph, etc.) that would do a good job of illustrating this poem.

Hurt Hawks

Robinson Jeffers

(Page 142)

1. There are two sections to this poem. What is the function of each? How do they differ? Notice how the poet uses the words "salvation," "redeemer," "God," and "merciful" in part I.

2. What does the poet mean by "I gave him the lead gift in the twilight"? What statement is the poem making? What is the tone of the poem? What could the hawk symbolize?

3. Can you say anything about what sort of man Robinson Jeffers was from this poem? What did he admire? What did he despise? What did he think about the societies of men?

4. Robinson Jeffers lived on a wild stretch of the California Coast in Big Sur (south of Carmel, California) in a house that he built himself out of native stones. Do you think a person who lived in New York City, Los Angeles, or any other large city could have written this poem? Even if they had had the actual experience of the relationship with the hurt hawk on a country vacation?

5. Can you put your finger on what it is about this poem that makes it what it is?

I Think I Could Turn and Live with Animals

Walt Whitman

(Page 143)

1. Whitman, like Robinson Jeffers in *Hurt Hawks,* is expressing his feelings about "civilized" man through nature. What doesn't he like about the habits of man? What does he say nature is in relation to man? Is he accurate about nature? Do animals live like he says they do?

2. What is Walt Whitman advocating here? What is he implying that man should do?

3. Compare Whitman's poem with *Hurt Hawks.* What are their similarities? What are their differences?

4. Look over the poems in this anthology that deal with nature. Is there a common theme throughout them? Why are poets so concerned about man's relationship to nature? Why do you think they feel nature is so important?

it is so long since
my heart has been with yours

e. e. cummings

(Page 144)

1. cummings uses words in unique and often surprising ways:

   "your mind has walked into / my kiss"
   "whittles life to eternity"
   "skillfully stuffed memories"
   "separating selves"

   What picture is he painting here with his words? What is the relationship described?

2. How does the poet see this love relationship affecting the rest of both their lives? Describe how the poet uses language to touch us rather than just tell us about this love.

3. Write a poem about love where you use images (visual, sensual, musical pictures) to make a poem that does more than just describe the experience. In other words, look for concrete things such as taste, or smell, or some visual things that will communicate more than just how you feel emotionally.

The Horse Chestnut Tree

Richard Eberhart

(Page 145)

1. Read the poem and then write out in a few sentences what happened. Is there a deeper meaning to this poem than the surface story? What do you think the poet is trying to say about man's role in the universe? Why are we "outlaws on God's property"? You might be wise to look in the Bible for the answer to that question; once again, have your reference librarian assist you in your search.

2. All but the last seven lines of the poem are narrative (i.e., they tell a story). What is their function? Do they change the tone? How?

3. Locate a copy of Robert Frost's *Birches* and then compare these two poems in relation to the way the two poets tell an essentially similar story. Which do you prefer? Why?

The End of the World
Archibald MacLeish
(Page 146)

1. What is an "armless ambidextrian"? What are "canceled skies"? Did you notice that this is a sonnet? What happens in the octave? What happens in the sestet?[44] What comment does the second part of the poem make on the first?

2. Notice the use of color imagery in the sestet, the contrast between white and black. What does this accomplish?

"Truly we can only allow our paintings to speak"
Jean Pumphrey
(Page 147)

1. If you do not know the paintings of van Gogh, this poem cannot mean too much to you. Art is a way of perceiving that which is shared by people all over the world. Here the poet refers to many paintings by Vincent van Gogh, a Dutch painter of the nineteenth century. If you don't know his work, get a book of his paintings and drawings. Be sure to look up the paintings mentioned in the poem—*Harvest, The Evening,* and *Potato Eaters.* There are other references within the poem to more of van Gogh's paintings and drawings. Can you locate them? This research is required because without the experience of van Gogh too much is lost from the poem.

2. Now that you have seen van Gogh paintings and drawings, what do you think of Jean Pumphrey's descriptions of them? Does she capture them on paper? What is the poet stating about van Gogh?

3. Now try experiencing this poem in another way. Try reading this poem backward (i.e., last line first, through to first line). Yes, you read correctly —backward. Jean Pumphrey read this poem both ways at a poetry conference and amazingly enough it made just as much sense either way. An extraordinary experience. A very unusual poem. Does the poem still make sense? Which way do you prefer it? Why?

---

[44]In a sonnet, the *octave* (first eight lines) sets the scene and the *sestet* (final six lines) makes some comment on the scene. The first line of the sestet is called the *volta* (Italian for "turn"), which is the pivot point of the poem. There is a turn in thought, for example, from a problem to a solution or from a question to an answer.

Holy Sonnet X
Death, be not proud
John Donne

(Page 149)

1. What does the poet mean by "poppy or charms . . .", "Thou'rt slave to fate, chance, kings, and desperate men," and "Why swell'st thou"?

2. This is an expression of John Donne's Christian faith in eternal life. What makes this such a memorable poem? (It is memorable, for sure, since we are reading it almost 350 years after it was written.) What does Donne do to make the thought—belief in life beyond death—come alive as poetry?

3. This poem is also a sonnet. It seems that sonnets, like all poems, often are written about love and death. Why would you say that love and death are such constant topics of poetry?

4. Donne addresses death directly as if death could be spoken to as a person. This is a literary device called *apostrophe,* that is, a direct address to an abstract person, inanimate object, or abstraction as though it were alive. Why would you think this device came into use? How does it increase the poem's effect on you?

Innocence
Thom Gunn

(Page 150)

1. What does the poet refer to when he says, "Culture of guilt and guilt's vague heritage"? What is like a "bud's tipped rage"? What does he mean by "The egotism of a healthy body"?

2. Do you sense the use of irony here? Is what is meant different from what is said? In other words, what does the poet say directly and what do you think the poet means to imply?

3. How would you describe a person that would fit the line, "No doubt could penetrate, no act could harm"?

4. Why is the title of this poem *Innocence?*

5. If you have doubts about the poet's attitude, apply his description to a Nazi soldier in World War II. Does that make your attitude toward the person described different? How?

The World Is Too Much with Us

William Wordsworth

(Page 151)

1. Who was Proteus? Triton? Describe the poet's attitude toward paganism and Christianity. What is he saying about the condition of people? What does he see wrong? What can correct this failing?

2. This is a sonnet divided in the traditional way. How does seeing that help you hear what is going on in the poem? What change takes place at the *volta* (see footnote 44).

3. Scan the rhyme scheme. Is it different than most of the other poems in this anthology? In what way?

Full Sky

Jules Supervielle

(Page 153)

1. Reading this poem is like being caught in a revolving door; you go around and around and eventually go out some way other than the way you came in. Try to follow the turns, get dizzy, and enjoy the ride. Can the poet tell us something by making a game for us to play, like a child's "creative play-thing" whereby a child thinks he's playing with wooden blocks but all the while is learning how to recognize numbers by trying to fit funny-shaped blocks through the proper holes)? If that is so here, what is the game you are being taught? If you were taken for a ride, where would the poet take you?

Truth

James Hearst

(Page 154)

1. Pay attention to the title of this poem. Is "truth" the subject of the poem? What is the experience being described here? What sort of person is the speaker?

2. This poem can be read on two levels: the literal and the figurative.[45] Does it make sense on the literal level? What figure of speech is used throughout the poem?

3. How does the poem relate to the quote from the Bible, "I have learned by experience" (Genesis 30:27) and the old cliché, "Experience is the best teacher"? When you are seeking truth, can you rely on your friend's or relative's opinions or experiences? What does the poet believe about this?

Icarus
Edward Field

The New Icarus
Vassar Miller

To A Friend Whose Work Has Come To Triumph
Anne Sexton

(Pages 155–157)

Themes appear in literature and occur over and over again from one culture to another. Often the themes take the form of mythical tales, which become very widely (occasionally universally) known. Since many people know about them, people feel comfortable making reference to them and often use the stories to express their own feelings about the themes.

Icarus is several themes tied together. Before you try to get into these poems, go to the library and read about the myth of Icarus and his father Daedalus and the Labyrinth and the Minotaur. They're fascinating stories.

We use the names given these myths by the Greeks (most myths occur only slightly changed) because the literature of the Greeks was the foundation for much of our Western culture. It is part of what has been taught in schools and the basis for transcultural communication among the "educated." Because for so long all educated people studied much the same things, an educated person from France had a mutual basis of communication for discussion with an educated person from Italy or England. Now we all have TV, which would be okay except that so far so much of it is ridiculous. But even in this age of TV, the ancient myths somehow survive.

---

[45]*Literal* means what actually happened without exaggeration or interpretation—the facts; *figurative*, the opposite of literal, means representation by using a figure of speech.

They survive because they are alive, because in stories about gods and heroes they are talking about man and asking the questions men still ask: How far should I allow my ambition to take me? How high should I fly? Is it better to stay a little lower and have a longer flight or burn out in a rush of flame? These are human questions, questions we all face. That is why poets are so interested in them: Poets are human and are living and having dilemmas and successes and failures, and they like to make up poems and songs to give some form to their experiences.

1. What are the three poets' attitudes toward life as expressed in relation to the Icarus myth? How do they feel about life and how do they *use* the myth to express their feelings? Describe how their choice of words emphasizes their respective attitudes.

2. What is the tone of each poem? Are they different? How?

There Was a Child Went Forth

Walt Whitman

(Page 159)

1. What do you think the child symbolizes in the poem? Is this poem about one child? Why doesn't the poet ever describe the child physically?

2. How are William Wordsworth's line "The Child is father of the Man" and Donne's lines (below) related to Walt Whitman's theme in *There Was a Child Went Forth?*

> No man is an island, entire of itself; every man is
> a piece of the continent, a part of the main; if a
> clod be washed away by the sea, Europe is the less,
> as well as if a promontory were, as well as if a manor of thy
> friends or of thine own were; any man's death diminishes me,
> because I am involved in mankind; and therefore never send to
> know for whom the bell tolls; it tolls for thee.
>
> *Devotions 17*

3. Notice how Whitman uses the article "the" and the conjunction "and" to begin many of the lines of his poem. Is it effective?

The Garden of Love

William Blake

(Page 161)

1. In his *Proverbs of Heaven and Hell,* Blake wrote "He who desires but acts not, breeds pestalence." Does that agree with what he says here? Explain.

2. Do you think Blake is against Christianity or against what he sees as a perversion of it? How can you tell that from this poem or any other Blake poems you know?

A Poem to Delight My Friends Who Laugh at Science-Fiction

Edwin Rolfe

(Page 162)

1. Write down the meaning of "early-Chirico landscapes," "conscripts," "seconal," "bicarb," "roisterers," and "Normandies."

2. From what you know from our earlier discussion, explain the reference to Icarus.

3. Explain the title. What would this narrative poem say to the person who laughs at science fiction?

4. This poem attempts to make a point. What is it?

A Dirge

Percy Bysshe Shelley

(Page 164)

1. What does "dreary main" mean? What is the rhyme scheme? What effect do the three rhymes in lines five, six, and seven have on the poem; that is, how does that shift the emphasis?

2. Relate this poem to the mood of *A Poem to Delight My Friends Who Laught at Science-Fiction.*

Young and Old

Charles Kingsley

(Page 165)

1. What are the two main divisions of this poem? Does the division of form match the division in meaning? What is said in the first stanza and what is said in the second?

2. What does "And every dog his day" mean?

Dolor

Theodore Roethke

(Page 167)

1. What does "dolor" mean? What is "silica"? What is "tedium"? What experience is Roethke appraising here? Have you ever experienced the same thing?

2. How does the poet fill in the picture? In other words, how does he construct this poem to affect you?

Do Not Go Gentle into That Good Night

Dylan Thomas

(Page 168)

1. If you want to get the full effect of this poem, listen to a voice recording of Dylan Thomas reading it. He had a wonderful voice, and it added an extra dimension to his works.

2. Do you feel that this poem was really written to his dying father? Describe the death experiences of certain types of men (e.g., "wise men," "Good men," etc.) as envisioned by the poet.

3. This poem is written in the French form called the *villanelle* (see footnote 43). Can you trace the characteristics of the form?

4. Can you think of any other poems in which death has been compared to night?

5. What is the poet's attitude toward death?

Tombstone with Cherubim

Horace Gregory

(Page 169)

1. What is "Lesbian serenity"? Where is "Michigan Boulevard"? What is "rococo"? Paraphrase this poem and compare your words with the poem. What is missing?

2. What is the tone of this poem? What does the title mean? (When you look up the word "cherubim" in your dictionary, be sure you look at all the meanings listed.)

3. What do the last lines, "Disconnect the telephone; / cut the wires" mean to you?

r-p-o-p-h-e-s-s-a-g-r

e. e. cummings

(Page 170)

1. It will help you decipher this poem if you think of it as an anagram.[46] Consider it a game. Can you make some order out of all those letters? Use the clues that e. e. cummings gives you. Once you've *really tried* to make some sense out of the unusual typography, look below for a fairly accurate interpretation of the poem.

   A grasshopper who, as we look up (now in the midst of gathering Grass into the Hopper), leaps, arriving in the hopper with the grass, to rearrangingly become: grasshopper.

2. Try writing your own poetic anagram. Is it difficult to compose one?

The Applicant

Sylvia Plath

(Page 171)

1. What is "poultice"? What does the poet mean by poultice? To what are the lines "But in twenty-five years she'll be silver, / In fifty, gold" referring?

---

[46]An *anagram* is a transposition of the letters of a word or sentence to form a new word or sentence.

2. What is Sylvia Plath writing about? In order to help you answer this question, think about the following: Who is the applicant? For what job is she applying?

3. Does the line "Will you marry it . . .?" clarify anything for you?

4. Do you agree with the comment that the poet is making? Why?

5. What is the tone of the poem?

Her Story

Naomi Long Madgett

(Page 173)

1. This poem seems to be the story of a woman's dreams and/or expectations at odds with her physical appearance and the limited role the world allows her. Describe her situation in each of the three stanzas.

2. Compare this situation to the situation in Sylvia Plath's *The Applicant*. Do you feel one woman's outcry more strongly than the other's? Why? List some ways in which they are similar. List some ways in which they differ. Does either of the poets pose an alternative solution?

Dover Beach

Matthew Arnold

(Page 174)

1. To whom is the poem addressed? Discuss the tone of the poem. Is it one of complete despair? What relation in regard to theme and tone do you find between this poem and Wordsworth's *The World Is Too Much with Us*?

2. How is nature presented in the first six lines of the poem? Is there a shift in the poem's tone after this? How does the speaker's *sight* of the sea differ from his sense of the *sound* of the sea? What is the role of the sea imagery? Why do you think the poet shifted the imagery in the last three lines of the poem?

Ode

William Wordsworth

(Page 175)

Since this is the longest poem in the book, it might be wise to look at some of Wordsworth's shorter poems first. Read *The World Is Too Much with Us* and *My Heart Leaps Up* and try to grasp a few of his central ideas or themes. Reading a long poem demands a slightly different sort of approach. Read the poem straight through—even if you get lost. Then reread each stanza *carefully* until you get its special feeling. Try to figure out what idea or theme is contained in each stanza. Finally, read the entire poem and put it all back together again. With a great poem, you can do this a hundred times and learn more about it each time.

1. Here are some more suggestions and some questions to help you unravel the poem: Look up all the words in the title and the poem that you do not understand. For example, what is an "ode"? Pay close attention to the epigraph.[47] What does Wordsworth mean "The Child is father of the Man"? Notice that he used capital letters on "child" and "man." Why do you think he did this?

2. Wordsworth addresses the child as "Thou best Philosopher," "Mighty Prophet," and "Seer blest." What is the poet inferring about children? What does he believe an adult loses as he grows older? Do you agree with him?

3. A sense of loss predominates in the first eight stanzas. What does the poet fear that he has lost? Beginning with the ninth stanza, how does the mood of the poem suddenly shift?

4. Reread these lines:

   Though nothing can bring back the hour
   Of splendour in the grass, of glory in the flower;
   We will grieve not, rather find
   Strength in what remains behind;

What is the poet trying to tell us about old age? Is he optimistic or pessimistic about it? What are his views on childhood?

5. There are a great many images of light and sound in this poem. Locate as many of them as you can. Do they help you see the structure in the poem? How?

---

[47]An *epigraph* is a suitable quotation at the beginning of a book, poem, and other writings.

Sensorium

We are not including any suggestions or questions
for the poems in the "Sensorium" section because we
want you to try to explore them without any guidance
from us. Read them carefully and try to *feel*
something while you are doing it. Notice each
poem's tone, imagery, rhythm, choice of words, and
sound. Then try to comprehend the poet's statement.
But first and foremost, feel something about the
poems before you begin to analyze them.